EXTRA INNINGS WITH THE VOICE OF SUMMER

ERNIE HARWELL

Credits

Editor	Kevin Bull
Designer	Ryan Ford
Copy editors	David Darby, Shelly Darby and the Free Press sports staff
Photo editor	Diane Weiss
Cover	Rick Nease
Photo imaging	Rose Ann McKean
Project coordinator	Steve Dorsey
Sports editor	Gene Myers
Special thanks	Matt Cammarata, Rick Cole, Laurie Delves, Bill Elwell, A.J. Hartley, Dan Loepp, Tim Marcinkoski, Stephen Mounteer, Drew Sharp and S. Gary Spicer Sr.

Detroit Free Press

615 W. Lafayette Blvd.
Detroit, MI 48226

OTHER FREE PRESS BOOKS BY ERNIE HARWELL

- Ernie Harwell: Life After Baseball
- Ernie Harwell: Stories from My Life in Baseball
- Ernie Harwell: Breaking 90

OTHER FREE PRESS TIGERS BOOKS

- Century of Champions
- Corner to Copa
- The Corner
- Roar Restored

 To order any of these titles, go to **www.freep.com/bookstore** or call **800-245-5082.**

For my fans

Thank you for your loyalty and
continued support.

Table of contents

Introduction

BY DREW SHARP

The first time I met Ernie Harwell, he introduced himself to me.

Shouldn't it have been the other way around? I was a first-year columnist with the Detroit Free Press in 1999 and he was ... well ... he was Ernie Harwell.

This was the voice of my childhood, a member of every native Detroiter's extended family, a source of comfort and optimism through the vibrant images he conveyed through decades of Tigers' radio broadcasts. And there was that distinctive baritone saying how he wanted to meet one of his favorite columnists.

I initially looked around to see if he was talking about somebody else.

Let's just say, I could've flown home that night without need of an aircraft.

He's too modest to understand the impact he has had on so many people simply through the sheer sincerity of his spirit. They don't erect statutes for that, but it's nonetheless the greatest legacy any of us can leave behind.

Ernie would often e-mail me, saying how much he liked a column. And the first reaction for some might be that it's a nice gesture, but he's a radio man. But Ernie always loved the written word. He

was a sports writer for the Atlanta Constitution
and also contributed to the Sporting News, which
back in that day in the 1940s, was baseball's biblical
tome.

Ernie is a great writer, explaining why he was a
great broadcaster. It's all about communicating
with your audience. His advice was invaluable to a
young columnist finding his voice. Like everything
else, Ernie kept it simple. Just tell the story. Let the
progression of the details reported spur the readers' emotions, be it excitement or exasperation.

Don't just "be yourself," he told me, but more
importantly, "be comfortable with yourself."

There may be no truer pearls of wisdom from a
man very contented with the indefatigable strength
he draws from his family, friends and faith.

Ernie remains Detroit's communal uncle. He
symbolized home and the reassurance that embod-
ies. It didn't matter if you were driving several hundred miles away. When nightfall came and the radio
signals bounced just right, you could still clearly
catch him sitting in amazement at Mark Fidrych's
1976 rookie season or the Tigers racing to their 35-
5 start in 1984.

And, suddenly, you're transported back to your
back porch with your brother on a summer's
evening when your only concern as an 8-year-old
was whether Al Kaline could recover from his broken arm in time to play in his first World Series in
1968.

We'll always cherish the stories Ernie told on the

radio.

But there's also a treasure of written tales spun that we'll appreciate just as much.

A farewell address

Ernie Harwell addressed the fans and the Tigers organization in the middle of the third inning of Detroit's home game against Kansas City on Sept. 16, 2009:

"Thank you very much. We don't want to be penalized now for the delay of the game, but I do want to express my feelings here. It's a wonderful night for me. I really feel lucky to be here, and I want to thank you for that warm welcome.

"I want to express my deep appreciation to Mike Ilitch, Dave Dombrowski and the Tigers for that video salute and also for the many great things they've done for me and my family throughout my career here with the Tigers.

"In my almost 92 years on this earth, the good Lord has blessed me with a great journey. And the blessed part of that journey is it's going to end here in the great state of Michigan.

"I deeply appreciate the people of Michigan. I love their grit. I love the way they face life. I love the family values they have. And you Tiger fans are the greatest fans of all. No question about that. And I certainly want to thank you from the depth of my heart for your devotion, your support, your loyalty and your love. Thank you very much, and God bless you."

GIVEN AT COMERICA PARK ON SEPTEMBER 16, 2009.

KIRTHMON F. DOZIER

Ernie Harwell thanks the Tigers organization and the fans during a tribute at Comerica Park. There were tears, but none from Harwell.

$$\text{---}(1)\text{---}$$

TALES OF THE TIGERS

ERNIE ON THE MIKE:

It's two for the price of one for the Tigers. **"**

ON THE TIGERS TURNING A DOUBLE PLAY

Mechanical Man skips a gear

Only once — in 1949 — has a Baseball Hall of Fame inductee been the victim of a scathing newspaper attack, instead of being extolled on induction day.

That victim was Tigers second baseman Charlie Gehringer.

The attack came from Shirley Povich of the Washington Post. His motive stemmed from another first — Charlie's refusal to attend his own induction.

"I take no satisfaction in having cast one of the votes ... to install Charlie Gehringer in baseball's Hall of Fame," wrote Povich. "When they unveiled the plaques of the five new installees, the guy didn't even show up. ... Gehringer's office in Detroit gave as his excuse 'pressure of business.' He is a manufacturer's agent and couldn't tear himself away ... to accept his new honors personally. ...

"He might have found time to detach himself for a few hours to be on the scene when baseball was finding a niche for him among its immortals.

"Baseball was pretty good to Gehringer. ... It opened a highly profitable career for him. He was the best second baseman of his time and the highest paid. He collected $15,000 in World Series checks alone.

A 13-foot, steel statue of Charlie Gehringer stands alongside five other statues of Detroit Tigers Hall of Famers beyond the outfield at Comerica Park. The Mechanical Man, as he was nicknamed for his consistency, hit above .300 in 14 of his 19 seasons as the Tigers' second baseman.

DAVID P. GILKEY

"They gave a day for him in Detroit. ... Among the gifts was a check for $10,000 from club owner Walter O. Briggs Sr. Gehringer left baseball as one of its most honored players, certainly one of its wealthiest.

"Hundreds of former players on the fringe of greatness would have gone a-running to Cooperstown to be honored with a niche there. It is still the highest tribute the game can bestow. Of course, there is no cash award."

In writing his bitter attack, Povich didn't take time or effort to discover why Gehringer missed his induction. There was a reasonable explanation. Charlie was getting married in California to a lovely lady named Josephine Stillen. Their wedding plans had been finalized long before the Hall of Fame picked a conflicting induction date.

Charlie's close friend and former teammate, Marv Owen, was his best man. Marv and his wife, Vi, arranged for the Gehringer wedding in Santa Clara, Calif. However, when reporters found out about it, the betrothed couple escaped to San Jose for a quiet, private ceremony.

On her honeymoon, Jo first read the critical article about her new husband.

"I was flabbergasted," she said. "Of course, Charlie wanted to attend his induction, but we couldn't change plans after the Hall of Fame had picked a conflicting date. I couldn't understand Povich writing on a subject he knew nothing about."

After learning the facts, Povich personally apologized to the Gehringers and wrote a retraction. Over the years, Shirley and his wife became close friends with Charlie and Jo.

"At the meetings of the Hall of Fame Veterans committee, I would always remind Povich about that article," Jo said. "And all of us would have a good laugh about it."

ORIGINALLY PRINTED JULY 21, 2008.

ASK ERNIE!

ERNIE HARWELL ANSWERS READERS' QUESTIONS

NOT-QUITE INSTANT REPLAY

Q When I started listening to Tiger games in the late '40s they were re-created from telegraph information but sounded like the announcer was at the game. Please discuss how this re-creating was done.

A All away games in the majors were re-created until 1946, when the Yankees became the first to send their announcers on the road. After the first half of the '48 season, the Brooklyn Dodgers began to do their road games live. However, on a Dodger off-day, Red Barber and I re-created Cub games (the Cubs and Dodgers had the same sponsor, Old Gold cigarettes) from the WMGM studios in Manhattan.

By the mid-1950s, all major league clubs had discarded re-creations. The last team to go live was Pittsburgh.

In a re-created broadcast, the announcer became more of an actor than announcer. For example, the telegraphic report would read: "Granderson up. B1W....S1C....FOGS (foul over the grandstand). Out, short-to-first." From that, the announcer enhanced the details. He would describe — with full use of his imagination — the mannerisms of the pitcher, how the infielders and outfielders were set up, the batter's stance, the type of pitch and other details.

If the wire broke down, the announcer had to fill the delay with ad libs — most of them fanciful. Maybe a dog running on the field, or an argument, which never happened, or he might have the batter foul off 15 pitches. When President Ronald Reagan was a sports announcer at WHO Des Moines, he broadcast games of the Chicago Cubs and White Sox but never left Des Moines.

Questions remain about fake diary

Ty Cobb's diary didn't reach the literary stature of the diary of Samuel Pepys. Neither did it reflect the historical significance of Anne Frank's diary, but it had achieved a place of honor in the Baseball Hall of Fame Museum at Cooperstown.

That place of honor no longer exists. The Cobb diary is a fake and will forever be relegated to the archival basement in Cooperstown.

Brad Horn, spokesman for the Hall of Fame, issued this statement: "We have found that the 1946 Ty Cobb diary is an unreliable source, not representative of an authentic Ty Cobb artifact. Our suspicions have been confirmed by the FBI statement that 'the written entries are not consistent with the natural writing style of Tyrus R. Cobb.' The document has not been on display at the Museum since 2001, but will remain a part of our library collections. It will no longer be available as a research document."

The diary was part of a 200-item donation in November 1998 by Major League Baseball from the Barry Halper collection. Ted Spencer, then curator of the Hall of Fame, selected the items before the Sotheby auction of the Halper Collection for $21.8 million.

Ty Cobb, who like Ernie Harwell was born in Georgia, won 12 American League batting titles and retired with 4,191 hits in his career.

1906 FILE PHOTO

Horn said the FBI report was not available. Also, Spencer would not be available for an interview.

I first heard suspicions about the Cobb diary from Ron Keurajian of Oxford, Mich., an outstanding authority on forgery in the field of baseball autographs.

Ron had read an article about the item in the Summer 2007 edition of Memories and Dreams magazine, published by the Hall of Fame. The article, written by HOF historian Russell Wolinsky, reproduced several pages of the diary and detailed Cobb's golfing exploits. Keurajian phoned Wolinsky, requesting a copy of the artifact. Wolinsky told him, "I can't photocopy it for you because it is fragile and priceless."

"I remember telling him," said Ron, "that it was not priceless and it was an amateurish forgery."

In December 2008, Keurajian contacted Spencer. His call had been prompted by another magazine article that represented the Cobb diary as being authentic. Spencer was more responsive, saying he planned to send the diary to the FBI for further investigation.

Now, we get the official word that the once-treasured artifact is indeed fraudulent.

Here is Keurajian's analysis of the Cobb diary:

"The quality of the forgery is rudimentary, at best. It is far from being well-executed, as the hand evidences unsteady lines and the handwriting seems almost child-like. The entries appear contrived. For example, there is one about Joe DiMaggio which states 'he can't putt for big money' and another entry states 'also drinking too much.' Anybody who has ever read Cobb's writings knows that he would not write in such a fashion. Cobb was well-versed in the art of the written word and would never write crude comments such as these."

The Baseball Hall of Fame and its president, Jeff Idelson, should be commended on their decisive action. By admitting that the Cobb diary is an unreliable source, they have fulfilled their responsibility as a history museum to maintain the public trust.

However, the story is still incomplete. Many questions remain. Halper can't answer them because he died on Dec. 18, 2005. The FBI will not permit the Hall to release details of the report, or names or divisions of those involved in the inquiry.

Who was the forger? How did he con Halper into buying the diary? Did Halper have it authenticated? If so, by whom? Do any other copies of the fraudulent diary exist?

Someday, maybe we will have the answers.

ORIGINALLY PRINTED JULY 5, 2009.

ASK ERNIE!

ERNIE HARWELL ANSWERS READERS' QUESTIONS

THE GEORGIA PEACH

Q | Didn't you know Ty Cobb and spend some time with him?

A | Yes, I first met Cobb in 1941, my second year in broadcasting. When he was visiting his hometown of Royston, Ga., I suggested to my boss at WSB Atlanta that I go to Royston to interview Cobb. "He won't even give you the time of day," the boss said, but he finally relented. Cobb couldn't have been more pleasant. He was warm and friendly to me. Later, while covering the Masters, I had a long conversation with Ty. He told me a story about his early minor league career. I wrote that story for the Saturday Evening Post, my first article for a national magazine. After that, I was with Ty at old-timer luncheons and ballpark ceremonies in Baltimore and other cities. The so-called Meanest Man in Baseball was always great to me.

Feeling nostalgia for The Corner

Every day I see the love and affection people have for Tiger Stadium.

Detroit City Councilwoman JoAnn Watson said, "If it hadn't been for Tiger Stadium, I wouldn't be here." Her parents met there.

Many people have expressed tributes to the old park. Nostalgic letters are full of love and respect for the stadium.

Ms. Jean McMullen wrote that her mother — who worked at downtown Hudson's — spent her days off at the ballpark.

Betty J. Ghesquiere sat in the bleachers with her dad to watch the Tigers beat the Cubs in the 1945 World Series at Briggs Stadium.

Marge Colburn's Tigers were Greenberg, Cochrane and Gehringer, and she sent a photo of me with her in Traverse City.

Leslie Lazzerin had memories of watching the Green Bay Packers-Lions game on Thanksgiving.

The outpouring of love took me back to a letter I received in 2002 from 12-year-old Perrie Marie Douglas of Forrest, Ontario. At the age of 10, she had won a contest with this speech about Tiger Stadium:

"Last year, I lost a very special friend. She was 80 years old. She wasn't related to me, but she was a very important part of my family. We loved to visit her — even two hours away.

"This grand old lady played a big part in my life. She was born around the time the Titanic sunk. That was the start of a long and exciting existence. My great-great uncle Nick knew her from the time they were both young. She was gray the first time my grandfather met her. I don't remember the first time I met her because I was still a baby. It was an exciting event when we went to see her.

"She had a special charm that no one could resist. I am sure going to miss that grand old lady, Tiger Stadium."

I enjoy hearing from young fans like Perrie Marie, and old ones, about the park.

The demolition has heightened nostalgic feelings and love for Tiger Stadium. I share that great affection with all of you.

ORIGINALLY PRINTED AUGUST 4, 2008.

ASK ERNIE!

ERNIE HARWELL ANSWERS READERS' QUESTIONS

TIGER STADIUM RIGHTFIELD

Q I remember the lower deck of Tiger Stadium right-field being fenced off. The home runs to right had to be in the upper deck. If my memory is correct, which years were the lower deck in right fenced off?

A In two different seasons (1944 and 1961) the lower deck in rightfield had a screen extending 30 feet to the 10-foot overhang of the upper deck. The screen went 100 feet from the rightfield foul pole toward right-centerfield. A ball that would have been a home run into the lower deck in other seasons would hit the screen and bounce back onto the field in those two years.

TOMATOES AT THE CORNER

Q I seem to recall one of the Tigers grew tomatoes out in centerfield at the old Tiger Stadium. Can you recall whom it was?

A The tomato fancier was Billy Martin. When he managed the Tigers in 1971-73, he cultivated a patch of tomatoes at Tiger Stadium. Earl Weaver, the Orioles' manager, was doing the same in Baltimore. So, those two — always competitors — were at it again in another field, so to speak.

A few key numbers to remember

2

Only two Detroit pitchers — Mickey Lolich and Paul Foytack — have struck out 15 or more in a game. Lolich fanned 16 Angels and 16 Seattle Pilots in 1969. In 1972, he victimized 15 Red Sox. Foytack had a 15-strikeout game against the Washington Senators in 1956.

Justin Verlander of the Tigers struck out 13 in games against the Rangers and the Twins in 2009.

0

No Tigers left-hander has pitched a no-hitter, while five right-handers have turned in six no-no classics.

Virgil Trucks notched two in 1952. That was the year Virgil won five games and lost 19. It was also the first time the Tigers finished last in the American League.

23

Maybe you can win a few bucks with this question from Tiger lore. A certain Tiger shares the team career record for leadoff home runs and has the most walk-off homers. In other words, he is the top opener and closer in Tiger longball history.

The answer might surprise you: It's Lou Whitaker with 23 leadoff homers (tied with Curtis Granderson) and eight in the walk-off category.

.369

While we are in the question department — which Tiger records are the least likely to be broken? I know that we all say "records are made to be broken" and "never say never," but I have a couple of entries for the rarest Tiger feats.

First, I would pick Ty Cobb's .369 lifetime batting average. It has been listed as various other numbers, but the ballclub has settled on .369.

31

My other entry is Denny McLain's feat of winning 31 games in 1968. Dizzy Dean had won 30 for the Cardinals in 1934, the last time anybody had reached that mark. This means Denny's accomplishment has not been duplicated in the past 75 years. In modern baseball, no pitcher will have the chance to start enough games, stay in the game long enough or have the good fortune that befell McLain.

ORIGINALLY PRINTED JULY 19, 2009.

ASK ERNIE!

ERNIE HARWELL ANSWERS READERS' QUESTIONS

A GAME OF INCHES

 Has anyone ever copied Ty Cobb's "hands 6-inches apart" batting style? Why don't more people use this method?

 Cobb's style was a holdover from the 19th Century when that grip enjoyed wide popularity. It's hard to believe Ty's success didn't attract many imitators. But it didn't.

The most successful was Harry Heilmann, the Tigers' Hall of Fame outfielder. In Harry's early years he learned his batting skills from Cobb, his manager. Heilmann was the AL's last .400 hitter before Ted Williams came along in 1941. Heilmann's lifetime average was .342, same as Babe Ruth's.

Another fairly well-known star who used the "Cobb grip" was Rube Bressler, a Reds outfielder. In a 19-year career, he batted .301.

Take note of these interesting facts

◆ The Tigers' key is Curtis Granderson. He's their igniter. If he reaches base in the first inning, the Detroiters usually take the lead and eventually win the game. Despite his late-season batting slump, he is the best Tigers leadoff man I've ever watched.

◆ There was little noise about the introduction of the baseball replay. Thankfully, it hasn't been used often yet. I like the idea of confining the process to home runs. And I'm pleased the innovation has not interfered with arguments on other close decisions. We can still enjoy those on-the-field spats.

◆ The whining about the Twins' "long" 14-game road trip irked me. Each season, from 1904 till the major league expansion in the early '60s, teams took four trips of 12 to 20 games, and nobody complained.
And how about the Astros in 1992? The Republicans' August convention in Houston forced the team to make a 28-day, 26-game journey. Astros infielder Casey Candaele said: "I was hoping at the age of 50 or 60 to take a trip to see the USA, but I didn't expect it to happen when I was still playing."

Still, nobody will ever match the Cleveland Spiders in 1899, baseball's losingest team. So bad the home fans didn't want them, the Spiders spent 52 days on the road.

◆ Waiting for the playoffs, I'm reminded of a favorite Tiger moment. It happened in l987, when the underdog Twins defeated the Detroiters in the American League Championship Series. Minnesota was leading the series, 2-1. In the fourth game at Tiger Stadium, Detroit trailed, 4-3, in the sixth inning. It looked as if the home team might take the lead and turn the series around. But Darrell Evans, representing the tying run, was picked off third. He kneeled in the dirt for a long, embarrassing moment and then disappeared into his dugout.
The next afternoon, in Evans' first at-bat in Game 5, Tiger fans stood and gave him a rousing ovation, a true display of forgiveness.

◆ The Cubs made a great push in 2008 and whenever they make the World Series again, they will be the darlings of the media. Incidentally, attendance for the Cubs-Tigers fifth and final game of the 1908 World Series in Detroit is still the lowest in Series history, 6,210. It also remains the fastest Series game. Chicago took only 1 hour and 25 minutes to close out the Tigers, 2-0. Also, that Series saw a change in the umpiring setup. Two umps worked on the field while two others sat in the stands in case of an emergency. The following year all four umps were on the field.

ORIGINALLY PRINTED SEPTEMBER 29, 2008.

EXTRA INNINGS

GREATS OF THE GAME

66 ERNIE ON THE MIKE:

He sprays the ball all over. You have to guard all the exits against him. **99**

DESCRIBING A FAMOUS SINGLES HITTER

Rizzuto great on field, better in booth

Phil Rizzuto's death evoked cherished memories. The little guy's journey from a kid in Brooklyn to a star shortstop in the Bronx was an adventure. After 13 years on the diamond as a Yankees standout, he became even more famous as the team's broadcaster.

When Rizzuto started on the air, the bombastic Howard Cosell told him, "You'll never last. You look like George Burns and sound like Groucho Marx." Cosell was wrong. Rizzuto lasted 40 years and won the hearts of his listeners.

Openness and honesty were his strength. He was a natural. In the Yankees' booth he was the ex-player invading the turf of established professionals Mel Allen and Red Barber. They resented Rizzuto's off-hand approach to his job, but he didn't let their coolness bother him. He realized the public loved his asides about traffic problems, cannoli and pizza. Fans accepted the little guy as a friendly uncle, the colorful family character.

Rizzuto was a guy you loved to tease — a perfect foil for a trick or joke. I had a running gag with him whenever he came to Detroit. During these visits he always appeared on J.P. McCarthy's WJR morning show. Rizzuto would tell me: "I can't remember this guy's name. Is it J.P. or P.J.?" Sometimes I'd say, "It's J.P." Next time I'd say, "P.J." My continuous switching kept him in confusion.

Rizzuto's most recognized broadcast phrase was "Holy cow!" He claimed he had used it from his high school days. Harry Caray took exception, contending he was first to use it.

I told Rizzuto, "You're both wrong. The first to say 'Holy cow' was some ancient Tibetan monk, barbecuing back in fifth century."

My favorite Rizzuto story involved his habit of leaving a broadcast early to beat the traffic. At Yankee Stadium that usually meant the seventh or eighth inning. But this time the Yankees were in Detroit.

It was a Sunday afternoon game, June 24, 1962. The 22-inning battle lasted seven hours, the longest time for any game in Tigers history, and second in number of innings.

Jackie Reed won it for New York with a home run, the only homer in his three-year career.

Of course, Rizzuto was not there at the end. He had left the booth after six innings to catch a plane.

"I was still listening to my partner Mel Allen broadcasting the game as I turned into my driveway in New Jersey," he told me later.

I was on the Veterans Committee when it voted Rizzuto into the Hall of Fame in 1994. Ted Williams was the member who spearheaded the drive to elect the little guy. I supported Williams. Because of his diamond feats, Rizzuto deserved to be a Hall of Famer.

Yet he was even more famous and loved as the irrepressible broadcaster.

ORIGINALLY PRINTED AUGUST 27, 2007.

ASK ERNIE!

ERNIE HARWELL ANSWERS READERS' QUESTIONS

BASEBALL PHRASES

Q As a young boy, I heard you say "a man from Livonia caught that one." When did you begin to use that phrase and what memorable phrases from other broadcasters are you fond of?

A The first time I used that phrase was 1961, my second year here. A batter fouled a ball into the stands and, for no particular reason, I said, "he's probably from Saginaw (or some other city)." After that, I'd be walking through Tiger Stadium and somebody would stop me and say, "Hey, you haven't had a lady from Windsor catch a foul ball." So, that day a lady from Windsor would catch one. In Seattle, it would be Walla Walla. Or at Yankee Stadium, Tenafly, N.J.

I enjoy a lot of signature phrases from other broadcasters. For instance, "You can hang a star on that baby" (Jerry Coleman); "Going, going, gone" (Mel Allen); "Holy cow" (Phil Rizzuto, Harry Caray and others).

The pride of Crestline, Ohio

F ifty years ago, a brilliant young football prospect was barred from playing on his high school field.

But a baseball diamond will be named for him. It will be called Gates Brown Field in Crestline, Ohio.

Gates never reached his football potential, but he became baseball's premier pinch-hitter and a beloved Detroit sports hero.

Brown was such a sensational high school football prospect that even in his sophomore year, he attracted recruiters from Michigan, Notre Dame, Purdue and Ohio State.

Then, his life took a woeful turn. Bad behavior sent him to the Boys' Industrial School for juvenile offenders in Lancaster, Ohio, for seven months.

After his release, Gates returned to Crestline High, but officials refused to let him play football. Devastated that his dream of college stardom had vanished, he soon fell into trouble again, spending 22 months in the Mansfield Reformatory for robbery.

His football future became a lost cause, but while he was in prison, baseball rescued the disillusioned youngster. Tiger scout Pat Mullin signed Brown for a $7,000 bonus and Gates built an outstanding, 13-year big-league career — all with the Tigers.

JULIAN H. GONZALEZ

Gates Brown won a World Series as a player in 1968 and as a hitting coach in 1984, both times with the Detroit Tigers.

Now, his old football teammates want to demonstrate Crestline's pride, honoring Gates with a banquet and the dedication of the baseball diamond.

Among teammates formulating the plans are the Gottfried brothers and their cousins, the Harbaughs. Joe Gottfried is the University of South Alabama's athletic director. Brother Mike is a former Pitt football coach.

Jack Harbaugh was a football coach at Western Kentucky. His son John is the Baltimore Ravens coach and another son Jim is the football coach at Stanford and a former Michigan quarterback.

"We not only want to honor our old teammate for his baseball renown," said Joe Gottfried, "but also want to repay him for being deprived of his football future."

When I broadcast Tigers games, Gates was special. I realized how he had persevered to overcome his early struggles. He always conducted himself as a true gentleman.

I admired his love for his hometown and his pride in playing football there. I remember being in the Tigers' clubhouse with Gates and other Tigers, watching a film of the Gator racing for a touchdown in one of his high school triumphs.

Now, Gates can't race anymore, but the Crestline banquet will be a prideful triumph. He will break out his special smile when he sees the sign on Gates Brown Field and the historic marker with his picture and major league pinch-hit records.

Some of his Tiger teammates will attend the ceremonies: Mickey Stanley, Willie Horton, Tom Timmerman, Doug Gallagher and John Warden plan to let Gates know how much he means to them, to Detroit and to baseball.

They'll be pleased that Gates is regaining the good times he missed when his football dream vanished 50 years ago.

ORIGINALLY PRINTED APRIL 12, 2009.

ASK ERNIE!

ERNIE HARWELL ANSWERS READERS' QUESTIONS

HARRY HEILMANN

Q Tell us about Harry Heilmann, the Detroit Tigers player and sportscaster and Hall of Fame member. Why doesn't he have a statue at Comerica Park?

A Harry Heilmann had two great Detroit careers — 15 years as a player and another 17 years as a Tigers radio announcer. Harry was 19 when he made his Tigers debut in 1914. Starting as an infielder, he eventually moved to the outfield.

In his Hall of Fame career, Heilmann won American League batting titles four times with averages of .394 (1921), .403 ('23), .393 ('25) and .398 ('27).

In 1934, Heilmann began to broadcast Tigers games. He continued until he died of cancer on July 9, 1951, the day before the All-Star Game in Detroit. Ty Cobb visited Heilmann at his death bed and congratulated him on his election to the Baseball Hall of Fame. At the time, the statement was untrue, but Harry did enter the Hall of Fame in 1952.

Heilmann was highly acclaimed for his insightful broadcasts. His playing experience and his touch of humor enthralled listeners. He was a beloved Michigan sports figure. I don't know why there is no Heilmann statue at Comerica Park. He certainly deserves one.

Sherry Smith: The first pickoff artist

After three seasons with the Tigers and 20 in the major leagues, left-hander Kenny Rogers can list two outstanding career accomplishments: a perfect game against the Angels in 1994 and a major league-record 93 career pickoffs. And, with the Tigers in 2006, he has two American League playoff wins and a World Series victory.

Rogers' pickoff record intrigues me the most, because of a boyhood hero of mine, Sherrod (Sherry) Smith. He and my dad grew up together in Mansfield, Ga.

Smith was a left-hander with a great pickoff move — the best of his era.

You'll never read about Smith's pickoff prowess because pickoff records weren't kept until after 1974. But Smith's ability was legendary.

Babe Ruth said Smith "was the greatest pickoff artist who ever lived." Historian Dan Daniel wrote: "He had the most deadly move with a man on first. There were times when Sherry walked a dangerous batter deliberately, with the feel that he would lure his man off first. Even the fleet and crafty Max Carey could not run on Smith."

Umpire George Moriarty said this of Smith: "His throw to first was so uncanny and confusing that players dubbed it 'the miracle move.' For years they

JULIAN H. GONZALEZ

Former Tigers left-hander and All-Star Game starter Kenny Rogers holds the major league-record for career pickoffs with 93.

tried every means of timing it, but they were obliged to give it up as a futile task. To the runner, it appeared that Smith was looking right at the bat-ter. More than that, the runner was positive the pitcher had started his delivery to the plate. Then, in a jiffy, Smith would step toward first, uncork a throw close to the ground, and the first baseman would easily tag out the victim."

Smith pitched 14 seasons with Pittsburgh, Brooklyn and Cleveland. In 2,052 2/3 innings, he allowed only two stolen bases. In two seasons with Cleveland (1923 and 1926) he didn't make an error. Control? His career average for walks was 1.93 per nine innings.

The ironic twist to Smith's story is that he is most famous for a game he lost. Pitching for Brooklyn in Game 2 of the 1916 World Series, he lost, 2-1, in 14 innings to the Boston Red Sox — tied for the longest game in World Series history. The winning pitcher was Ruth, making his first World Series appearance. Each pitcher lasted the whole game, which took 2 hours and 32 minutes.

Smith and Ruth became close friends. Whenever Ruth came to Cleveland, he visited the Smith home where Sherry's wife, Addilu, stuffed the Babe with country ham and red eye gravy.

After his playing career, Smith returned to Georgia. In his final year in baseball, Smith managed the Macon Peaches.

In 1980, the Georgia Sports Hall of Fame honored Smith with a posthumous induction, a final salute to the all-time master of the pickoff.

ORIGINALLY PRINTED AUGUST 25, 2008.

ASK ERNIE!

ERNIE HARWELL ANSWERS READERS' QUESTIONS

BOBO NEWSOM

Q I believe Tigers pitcher Bobo Newsom once pitched both games of a doubleheader. If so, did he win both games?

A It has long been a myth that Bobo Newsom once achieved victories in both games of a Tigers doubleheader. Good story, but not true.

Newsom might have invented the story. After all, once when a reporter challenged Bobo's recitation of one of his records, the pitcher said, "Who you gonna believe, the record book or the guy who set the record?"

However, Bobo, in his 20-year career, did start four doubleheaders — two for the Browns, one for the Red Sox and one for the Philadelphia A's. In three, he pitched against the Philadelphia A's, winning one game and losing the other. In the fourth doubleheader, he started for the A's against the Tigers. It was another split, but Newsom was not the pitcher of record in either game.

Outfield greats have 20-20-20-20 vision

The historical magnitude of Curtis Granderson joining Willie Mays and Frank Schulte in baseball's 20-20-20-20 club among outfielders is overwhelming.

Reaching the 20 mark in doubles, triples, home runs and stolen bases has happened once about every 50 years.

Most fans know about Granderson, the up-and-coming superstar. Some know about Willie Mays, who retired years ago. Few have any knowledge of Schulte.

Mays was the greatest player I ever saw. He could hit for average and with power. He was a sensational outfielder and a talented runner.

Strangely enough, a terrible start in the majors almost wrecked his career. As a highly touted 19-year-old rookie, Mays hit .477 for Minneapolis in the American Association when the Giants brought him up in late May 1951. He failed to get a hit in his first 12 at-bats. Mays felt overwhelmed and lost his confidence.

Crying, he visited manager Leo Durocher in his office.

"Leo, I can't play up here," he said. "Send me back to Minneapolis."

"Settle down, Willie," Durocher said. "As long as

I'm manager here, you are my centerfielder. Relax and play your game. You'll be all right."

Mays recovered, batted .274 with 20 home runs and was named National League Rookie of the Year. But, without the support of his manager, Willie's story would have been entirely different.

Frank (Wildfire) Schulte spent most of his 15-year career with the Cubs, playing in four World Series. In 1911, Frank had his best season — 30 doubles, 21 triples, 21 home runs and 23 stolen bases. He hit for the cycle that year, and in another game homered and doubled in the same inning.

He led the NL in home runs in 1910 with 10, and when he did it again in '11, his 21 homers were hailed as an outstanding feat, since the total homer output for the rest of the team was 33.

Schulte's super season featured four grand slams (a record at the time) and earned him the MVP.

His other distinction was his nickname, acquired because of a lady and a horse. The lady was the great actress Lillian Russell. The Cubs were in Vicksburg, Miss., where Russell was starring in a play "Wildfire." She threw a party for Schulte and his Cubs teammates. In her honor, Schulte named one of his horses Wildfire. Eventually, Wildfire became his nickname.

ORIGINALLY PRINTED SEPTEMBER 17, 2007.

ASK ERNIE!

NO-HIT THE TIGERS

Q Who was the last pitcher to throw a no-hitter against the Tigers?

A The last man to no-hit Detroit was Randy Johnson of Seattle. He did it at the Kingdome on June 2, 1990.

The only pitcher to achieve a perfect game against Detroit was the White Sox's Charles Robertson, certainly not a world-beater. In his eight-year big-league career, he never reached the .500 mark in any one season. Yet, on April 30, 1922, Charlie turned in a perfecto at Navin Field.

BEST HITTERS

Q Whom do you send to the plate, bottom of ninth, two out, man on first and down by one run? Give us your top three or four picks.

A This is dangerous territory. I'm sure my answer won't settle anything. It will probably raise even more questions. But here it goes. My top pick would be Babe Ruth, the ultimate hitter. Then, it would be Ty Cobb, Willie Mays and Stan Musial.

BASEBALL PEOPLE

" **ERNIE ON THE MIKE:**

Some of the umpires who paid to get in disagreed with that call. "

WHEN FANS BOO AFTER A DISPUTED PLAY

A lone Tigers fan in the Lone Star state

Warren Bradley, an impressionist and comedian from Longview, Texas, has not missed a Tigers game in Texas since 1976.

But the last game he missed was a classic. Mark (The Bird) Fidrych outdueled Bert Blyleven, 3-2, in 13 innings.

"I had agreed to usher a girlfriend's wedding," Bradley said. "Two years later, I told her, 'If I'd known then what I know now, I wouldn't have missed that game.' By then a divorcee, she answered, 'If I had known then what I know now, I would have gone to the game with you.' "

Since then, Bradley has watched Tigers-Rangers games for 32 years — 173 consecutive games. He drives 150 miles from Longview to follow his heroes. Sometimes he stays in an Arlington hotel for the entire series, but often drives the 300 miles round-trip between games.

I've known Bradley since our first meeting in 1972, the Tigers' first year in Texas. We've become fast friends, sharing many lunches and dinners. My broadcast partners always enjoyed his wit and insightful comments.

Bradley's consistent attendance has gained him two more lifelong friends whom he met in the stands. They are Pete Costa, a realtor from Livonia, and Byron Hatch, a truck driver from Flint.

Bradley's parents once lived in Detroit, where his dad was a car salesman. Born in Longview, he became hooked on the Tigers in 1968 when his uncle Verlin Lively of Dearborn took him to his first game at Tiger Stadium. Since then, he has augmented his Arlington attendance record by attending many games in Detroit.

Bradley started as the Cal Ripken of Tigers fans when the Washington Senators moved to Texas in 1972 to become the Rangers.

How focused is Bradley on seeing Tigers games in Texas? Consider this:

On the first day of a job with Allied Finance Co., he got permission to leave early to catch a game.

Bradley won his way to the finals of a talent competition in 1999 at Shreveport, La., but gave up his chance for the title and a trip to Acapulco because the date conflicted with a Tigers game in Arlington.

His radio contract with a Longview station stated that Bradley would not work at any time the Tigers were in Arlington.

In 2007, he signed to do the opening act of The Salute to Jim Reeves Show in Branson, Mo., with the stipulation that he could leave when the Tigers were scheduled for a Texas appearance.

In his present job of driving for Hertz, he has an understanding that no assignment can keep him from a Tigers game.

Bradley continues to perform. He has opened shows for the Oak Ridge Boys and Neal McCoy. His specialty is impersonating famous voices — over 70 of them — from George W. Bush to Jeff Foxworthy.

Although a talented professional entertainer, Bradley's favorite act is watching his Tigers in Texas and keeping his streak alive.

ORIGINALLY PRINTED SEPTEMBER 15, 2008.

ASK ERNIE!

ERNIE HARWELL ANSWERS READERS' QUESTIONS

CAMDEN YARDS

Q Is Camden Yards in Baltimore still the standard for modern ballparks?

A To me, it is. I haven't seen all the parks, but baseball people tell me that Camden Yards is the retro park by which all others are measured. My favorite new one is Safeco in Seattle. It's outdoors, but can be covered in bad weather. It's downtown and beautifully constructed.

CATCHING THE BALL

Q In my time growing up, ballplayers were instructed to use both hands when catching a baseball, securing it from popping out of the glove. Why has baseball abandoned this practice?

A I remember the old sandlot cry, "Two hands for beginners." Today, the one-handed catch is almost universal. I asked Alan Trammell how he teaches young players to catch a ball. "My preference is the two-handed method," he said. "But I tell them to do it the way they feel most comfortable. And I always add, 'Just be sure you don't drop the ball.' "

Choice pays off for Tigers trainer Rand

Tigers head trainer Kevin Rand had begun a baseball coaching career when his life took a sudden twist.

A phone call from Stump Merrill, who would later manage the Yankees, did it. Then a minor league supervisor for the New Yorkers, Stump asked Rand if he would like to be the trainer for the organization's Ft. Lauderdale team.

"It was an absolute surprise to me," Kevin said. "I had known Stump when he was the assistant football coach at Bowdoin, where I played baseball four years. He knew I had a great passion for baseball and also that I had worked as assistant under Bowdoin trainer Mike Linkovich, who was in the National Athletic Trainers Association Hall of Fame."

When he got that phone call, Rand had graduated from Bowdoin College in Maine and had been coaching St. Joseph College's Division III baseball team.

"It was a tough decision," Kevin said. "At the age of 21, I was the youngest coach in the country and felt reluctant to take a chance on a sports training career. At that time, being a trainer was the furthest thing from my mind — I thought I'd always be teaching and coaching."

JULIAN H. GONZALEZ

Trainer Kevin Rand, right, and his crew were named staff of the year in '06 by the Professional Baseball Athletic Trainers Society.

After deep deliberation, Kevin decided to accept the job. "I felt I could learn more baseball that way," he said.

He joined the Ft. Lauderdale team in 1982, returning for two off-seasons to Bowdoin, where he honed his skills under his highly regarded tutor, Linkovich. He quickly moved up in the Yankees organization with stops at Albany and Columbus. His next promotion brought him the job of minor league head athletic trainer/rehabilitation supervisor. He spent four years in that position — his final four seasons in the Yankees organization.

In November 1992, Rand left the Yankees to join the Florida Marlins as assistant trainer. There he worked for his present boss, Dave Dombrowski. After nine years with the Marlins, Kevin joined the Montreal Expos for one year as assistant trainer.

"At the end of the season," Rand said, "I heard rumors that Russ Miller might leave the Tigers' head training job. Then I got a call from Dave Dombrowski. I accepted his offer to replace Russ."

Kevin likes it here in Detroit, and the Tigers like his expertise and professionalism.

President Dombrowski has high regard for his trainer.

"I've known Rand for 15 years," he said. "He is very knowledgeable, hard-working and intelligent. He is always willing to do anything to help our players and our organization."

In 2006, the Tigers training staff of Rand, Steve Carter and Doug Teter was named the staff of the year by the Professional Baseball Athletic Trainers Society. The next year Kevin entered the Maine Sports Hall of Fame — not as a player or coach, but as an outstanding trainer.

ORIGINALLY PRINTED MAY 5, 2008.

ASK ERNIE!

ERNIE HARWELL ANSWERS READERS' QUESTIONS

HOT POTATO HAMLIN

Q Luke (Hot Potato) Hamlin grew up in the Lansing area and played for the Tigers in 1933-34 and later became a 20-game winner with the Dodgers. One of his coaches was Babe Ruth. Why the nickname "Hot Potato"?

A That nickname was pinned on Hamlin because he juggled the ball (like a hot potato) while getting ready to pitch. Luke pitched in the majors for nine years, five of them with the Dodgers. He won 20 games for them in 1939, but later his manager, Leo Durocher, soured on Hamlin. When I broadcast for the Dodgers a veteran writer told me that once when Durocher saw an old campaign poster of the Abe Lincoln-Hannibal Hamlin ticket, he said: "That proves what a great man Lincoln was. He could even win with Hamlin on his team."

I was surprised that the earthy, street-smart Durocher knew about Hannibal, who had become so frustrated by lack of meaningful work as vice president that he enlisted as a private in the Maine Coast Guard while still in office.

Meet the authority on ball in Japan

B rad Lefton's short vacation in Japan became an extended career as an expert on Japanese baseball.

I met Brad when he came to Tiger Stadium to film a documentary about Seattle's Ichiro Suzuki several years ago. I caught up with him again and asked about baseball in Japan and the United States.

QUESTION: How did you get to be a guru on Japanese baseball?

ANSWER: It was completely unplanned. I had never studied the Japanese or their culture. But after I graduated from Washington University in St. Louis, a friend asked me to visit him in Osaka. I had planned a short vacation, but when I found myself mesmerized by the culture — and especially Japanese baseball — I extended my stay.

Because I had interned at KMOX radio while in high school and college, I wanted to do radio in Japan. I contacted Bob Costas. He said: "If you interview American players, I can use your work on 'Costas Coast to Coast.' " I talked with Bill Madlock, Matt Keough and other stars and began to get involved in the Japanese game.

I was lucky to be in Japan in 1995, the pivotal year in the Japanese-USA baseball story. That sea-

KIRTHMON F. DOZIER

Fans show their support for Ichiro Suzuki and the Seattle Mariners before a 2001 game against the Tigers at Comerica Park.

son, Hideo Nomo became the first Japanese player to become an American major leaguer — at least, the first as recognized by the Japanese themselves. Masanori Murakami had pitched in 1964-65 for the Giants, but because he did not go on his own volition, the Japanese don't consider him the first.

Another important event happened that year. Bobby Valentine came to Japan to manage the Chiba Lotte Marines, becoming the first ex-big-league manager to lead a team in Japan. By then, I was in TV, and did many Valentine interviews and stories.

Q: How do Japanese fans feel about their big stars leaving for the United States?

A: Some feel this exodus might result in the demise of Japanese leagues. Others don't. My own opinion is that the only way the sport can rise in Japan is for the Japanese stars eventually to measure up to the American players. Hopefully, they can do this and create an interest in a World Baseball Classic among all the nations.

Q: Which Japanese star in America is the most outstanding?

A: Ichiro. He is unparalleled both here and in Japan.

Q: Which Japanese big-leaguer gets the most coverage in Japan?

A: Ichiro, because he is the most consistent — always challenging records and heading for the Hall of Fame. He is the most-recognized of all Japanese players.

However, there are three others who attract major attention in Japan. Nomo had a tremendous following, even up until his final — but failed — comeback attempt at Kansas City (in 2008). Daisuke Matsuzaka, the Boston pitcher, is a hot product now. And Hideki Matsui, the Yankee slugger, draws unusual interest because he once played for the Yomiuri Giants, the team regarded as the Yankees of Japan.

ORIGINALLY PRINTED JUNE 9, 2008.

ASK ERNIE!

ERNIE HARWELL ANSWERS READERS' QUESTIONS

CHOOSING SIDES

Q Is there a rule that the home team always has the third-base dugout?

A There has never been such a rule. Dugout selection is based on the whim of the home team. Usually, the visitors get the first-base side, because in most parks it faces the sun. Sunken dugouts did not exist until the steel stadiums were built around 1910.

QUICK HITTERS

Q What's the record for fastest to 1,000, 2,000 and 3,000 hits?

A For this answer, we leaned on Freddie Berowski of the Baseball Hall of Fame Look-Em-Up Department. The first to reach the 1,000-hit mark in his career was Chuck Klein in his 683rd game. The 2,000 record-holder is Wee Willie Keeler, who did it in 1,270 games. And the ole Georgia Peach, Ty Cobb, is the 3,000-hit champion. He got number 3,000 in his 2,135th game.

ASK ERNIE!

ERNIE HARWELL ANSWERS READERS' QUESTIONS

KEEPING SCORE

Q Could you explain a little bit about the official scorer? I wonder how they are chosen, what qualifications they have, whether there is some sort of training?

A The history of this job goes back to the 1880s. At first, official scoring was very unofficial, with the writers keeping their own score. As late as the 1950s, official figures often differed from newspaper box scores, leading to a wait of weeks after the season for publication of the official averages.

I remember Dave Philley, an Orioles outfielder, playing the final game of the 1955 season in Detroit. Early in the game, his hit moved him above the .300 mark for the season. When Orioles manager Paul Richards heard the news from the press box, he granted Philley's request for an early departure. Three weeks later, Philley checked the average in his local paper, only to discover that he actually batted .299.

At one time, a friendly beat writer was the team's official scorer. Not anymore. With the commissioner's office now in charge, Phyllis Merhige, MLB senior vice president of club relations, does the choosing based on recommendations from each team's public-relations department. There is no training required.

At Comerica Park three scorers alternate. Chuck Klonke, one-time sports writer, is the veteran. The others are Dan Marowski and Ron Kleinfelter. As independent contractors, they are paid $135 per game.

Jerry Lewis makes camping fun

t started 25 years ago with an insignificant
Sporting News item.
Jerry Lewis, a Southfield clothing representative, saw that small article and had a big idea. He
developed it into the popular Tigers Fantasy Camp.

"The story concerned former Cubs catcher
Randy Hundley's fantasy camp," Lewis said. "It led
me to thinking how great it would be to mingle
with Al Kaline, Norman Cash or Mickey Lolich."

Lewis and retired Tigers catcher Jim Price had
become close friends while working for MichCon.
Lewis contacted Price, who liked the idea and
arranged a meeting with Tigers GM Jim Campbell.

"Jim endorsed our plan," Lewis said. "A terrific
boost. From its start in 1984, the camp has been a
tremendous success."

Soon, Lewis and Price developed their Sports
Fantasies Inc. into a thriving business. They
expanded into camps for the Red Wings and the
Pistons. By 1993, their yearly revenue had reached
half a million dollars.

In 1995, the Tigers assumed operation of the
camp. The club retained Lewis as consultant and
two years later brought him into the organization
as full-time director of the camp. Price — who with
Dan Dickerson broadcasts Tigers games on radio

— has continued to help Lewis and is one of the most popular camp leaders.

My first experience with the event provided a surprise. Jerry and Jim hired me to do video interviews with 60 campers. Based on experience with major leaguers, I anticipated two days' work. Surprise! The 60 interviews required less than three hours. Campers quickly lined up, showed me the name on their shirts and chatted three minutes.

After each interview, I said, "For being my guest, here's a pair of Florsheim shoes from Sibley's, Michigan's largest Florsheim dealer."

Before the fantasy camper left, he would say, "But Ernie, you didn't give me those shoes."

"You're right," I'd tell him. "But that's part of the fantasy."

Lewis' idea keeps growing. He now has two fantasy camps every winter, averaging 220 participants — including many women. Lady campers generally are the best athletes.

Lewis has developed his fantasy camps into summer camps at Comerica Park, alumni lunches, trips to other major league parks and batting practice at Comerica. Major League Baseball executives enhanced Lewis' national reputation when they selected him to conduct camps at All-Star Games. He received rave reviews for his expertise and professionalism.

Lewis and the Tigers Fantasy Camp have come a long way. And it all started when Jerry saw that article.

ORIGINALLY PRINTED AUGUST 20, 2007.

ASK ERNIE!

ERNIE HARWELL ANSWERS READERS' QUESTIONS

DOUBLE SWITCH

Q | **When did the double switch begin and what manager originated it?**

A For this answer, I called on the guru of baseball rule history, former American League umpire Jim Evans. Here is what he told me: "There are no records of the double switch prior to 1948. Lou Boudreau made the first one in 1948 while managing Cleveland. It was done once in 1950 by Browns manager Luke Sewell; once in 1951 by Tigers manager Red Rolfe. Increase in its use began in 1952. White Sox manager Paul Richards and others used it a total of four times. By 1967, the number of double switches had reached 132. High point in the switch was 505 times in 1998. The total in 2008 was 34. There is no definition of 'double switch' in the rule book. It is called 'multiple substitution.' "

BASEBALL STORIES

ERNIE ON THE MIKE:

A gentleman from Livonia caught that one.

ON THE FOUL BALL INTO THE STANDS

Seeing the 1943 Series as a Marine

M y first look at Yankee Stadium was Oct. 5, 1943. On a short leave from the Marines, I made my first visit to New York. I arrived in the big city at 2:30 a.m. without any idea where to stay. Coming out of Penn Station, I flagged a cab.

"Take me to some place where a serviceman can sleep," I told the cabbie.

"There's a big place at Columbus Circle," he said. "It's 50 cents a bed, but you'll be with seven hundred other guys."

I spent the rest of the night there, sleeping in my Marine uniform with my hand on my wallet.

The next afternoon, the Yankees and the Cardinals opened the World Series at Yankee Stadium. I left my cot early and headed for the Commodore Hotel, hoping to see the Cardinal players and other baseball people. I didn't find any players, but through the lobby strode the famous baseball commissioner, Kenesaw Mountain Landis, with his entourage.

I went up to the shaggy-haired, bent-over Landis and said, "Hi, Commissioner. How 'bout a ticket for the game today?"

He stared at me. "Hello, Marine," he said and kept on walking. I had discovered it wasn't true that a man in uniform could get almost anything free in New York City.

However, that bit of street wisdom was almost true at Yankee Stadium that day. When I got there, the ticket line was long, stretching two or three blocks around the stadium. Some of the folks in line spotted my uniform and yelled, "Hey, Marine, go to the front of the line." The ticket wasn't free, but that long line parted for me, and I didn't have to wait.

Yankee Stadium overwhelmed me. Yes, it was wartime baseball, but still exciting. The Yankees' Spud Chandler outpitched Max Lanier, the Cards' left-hander, in that opener, 4-2. New York went on to win the Series in five games. Each club still had big-name stars on their war-depleted rosters. Bill Dickey, Frank Crosetti, Joe Gordon and Charlie Keller were with the Yankees. The Cardinal stand-outs were Stan Musial, Marty Marion, Harry Brecheen, and Mort and Walker Cooper.

My next visit to Yankee Stadium was in the fall of 1948, when I announced an All-America Football Conference game between the Brooklyn Dodgers and the New York Yankees. In 1963, I returned there for my first World Series broadcast, the Yankees against the L.A. Dodgers.

I have experienced many thrilling moments at Yankee Stadium, but I still retain a most vivid memory of that first visit during World War II.

ORIGINALLY PRINTED JULY 7, 2008.

ASK ERNIE!

ERNIE HARWELL ANSWERS READERS' QUESTIONS

TAKE ME OUT ...

Q The song "Take Me Out to the Ball Game" ends: "for it's one, two, three strikes you're out at the old ball game." But was there a second verse? I think my dad many years ago would sing it.

A Your dad might have sung both verses. The structure of the famous song is verse, chorus, verse, chorus. In each verse Nelly Kelly asks her beau to take her out to the ballgame. 2008 was the 100th anniversary of this famous ballad — the third-most performed song in pop music history. Only "Happy Birthday" and "The Star-Spangled Banner" have been sung more than "Take Me Out to the Ball Game."

Manager changes can come quickly

The soonest managerial firing of all came even before Opening Day.

In 1954, after completing spring training in Arizona, the Cubs and the Orioles played each other as they rode the train together on their way home. Phil Cavarretta, who had been one of the most popular players for the Cubs, was the manager. He led the club to a seventh-place finish in 1953, his third year as Cub skipper. One of the stops on the train was Dallas, Cavarretta's hometown, where he'd be united with his family, and all his friends would come to the game to pay him tribute.

Phil didn't know it, but he was in for a surprise.

He left the traveling entourage a day early to spend time with his family, and when the two teams arrived in Dallas, the Cubs called a press conference.

Yes, you guessed it. At the press conference, team president Phil Wrigley told the baseball world that Cavarretta had been fired — in his own hometown. That was some two weeks before the start of the regular season — about as early as you can dump a manager.

Another early departure of a manager was voluntary.

Eddie Sawyer managed the Phillies to an eighth-

JULIAN H. GONZALEZ

Yogi Berra, left, and Jim Leyland each took teams in the American League and National League to the World Series as managers.

place finish in 1959. He began the 1960 season by losing on Opening Day. After the defeat, Sawyer announced his retirement. Asked why he was quitting, Sawyer replied, "I'm 49 years old, and I want to live to be 50."

Another manager who wanted to live longer and couldn't take it any more was Eddie Stanky, one of the four managers of the 1977 Texas Rangers. Eddie managed one game — his Rangers beat the Twins in Minnesota. When he returned to his hotel room in Arlington, Stanky phoned his wife, Dickie, to tell her he was quitting and coming home.

"Why are you quitting?" she asked. "You've managed only one game, and you won it."

"I don't want to manage anymore," he told her. "I can't stand these players."

Now comes the strangest of all manager firing/retiring stories. In 1964, Johnny Keane's St. Louis Cardinals won the National League pennant, and Yogi Berra led the Yankees to the American League title. Before the season ended, both clubs had decided to fire their managers after the season because neither team seemed destined to win a pennant.

Berra was fired soon after the World Series (won by the Cards, 4-3). Secretly, Keane had signed a contract to succeed Yogi as Yankee manager. Meanwhile, the Cardinals changed their minds about firing Keane. They scheduled a press conference to sign Keane to a new contract. Instead, Johnny fooled everybody by announcing that he was leaving to become the next Yankee manager.

ORIGINALLY PRINTED JUNE 16, 2008.

ASK ERNIE!

ERNIE HARWELL ANSWERS READERS' QUESTIONS

ZIPPED JACKETS

Q Why do managers Mike Scioscia of the Angels and Terry Francona of the Red Sox wear jackets zipped to the top? Aren't managers required to wear a uniform top?

A Managers are required to wear a uniform in the dugout. Francona zips up because he is always cold due to poor circulation. In 2008, an American League official confronted Francona on this issue. Terry said he was wearing a uniform under his jacket. Inspection proved that he was wearing a T-shirt. Francona and Scioscia are top-notch managers, but fall short in the fashion department.

Sparky, umpires share bond for life

Throughout baseball there has always been talk about respect for the game. Jim Leyland and his coaches talk about it — just as Sparky Anderson, Mayo Smith, Mickey Cochrane and others once did.

This is a story about respect.

Al Barlick was the sixth umpire to be inducted into the Baseball Hall of Fame. At the age of 25, he was one of the youngest to become a major leaguer, and he worked 33 distinguished years. When Sparky Anderson broke into the major leagues with the Phillies in 1959, Barlick was an established veteran.

The Phillies were playing a doubleheader at home. Barlick was the first-base umpire in the opening game. He made a call that cost the Phillies the game. Manager Eddie Sawyer was steaming. He was still steaming when the second game was set to begin. He was so hot that he refused to come to home plate to give his lineup to Barlick. From his dugout, Sawyer kept cursing the ump. Barlick walked toward the Phillies' dugout.

"One more word from you and you're outta the game," he warned. When Sawyer kept spewing invectives, Barlick tossed him.

As Sawyer made his way to the clubhouse, rook-

1984 PHOTO BY MARY SCHROEDER

Jim Evans restrains Sparky Anderson, who is protesting a runner interference call. The manager later admitted he was wrong.

ie infielder Sparky Anderson yelled, "He's right, Barlick. That goes for me, too."

Barlick whipped off his mask and started after Anderson. Sparky sneaked down the tunnel, but the umpire gave chase, roaring, "Young man, if I ever hear that kind of talk from you, you'll regret it the rest of your life."

In the third inning, Anderson came to bat for his
first time. He swung and missed the first two pitches. The next one came close, just off the outside
corner. It was a chance for the veteran ump to
teach the rookie a lesson. Instead, Barlick ruled it
ball one.

Sparky asked for time and stepped back from
the plate, "Mr. Barlick," he said, "from now on,
throughout the rest of my career you will have my
utmost respect."

That's not quite the end of the story. When
Sparky was managing the Reds, Barlick came to
him and said: "I have a protégé named Ed Vargo.
Take care of him and help me make him a good
umpire."

After Barlick retired and Vargo had become an
umpiring fixture, Vargo came to Sparky with a protégé named Bruce Froemming. The same conversation again. When Froemming retired after the 2007
season, he had worked a record 37 big-league years
and, at age 68, had become the oldest major league
umpire of all-time.

Respect for the game can last for generations.

ORIGINALLY PRINTED SEPTEMBER 13, 2009.

ASK ERNIE!

ERNIE HARWELL ANSWERS READERS' QUESTIONS

FINALES AT TIGER STADIUM

Q How many fans attended the final Tigers game and the final Lions game at Tiger Stadium?

A The attendance for the Tigers game on Sept. 27, 1999, was 43,356. Detroit beat Kansas City, 8-2. Highlights were Robert Fick's eighth-inning grand slam and Todd Jones' final strikeout pitch.

The Lions lost their finale to Denver at Tiger Stadium, 31-27, on Nov. 28, 1974. Attendance was 53,314. Something notable was a career-ending injury sustained by former Heisman winner Steve Owens.

ON THE BLACK?

Q I have heard broadcasters refer to a pitch that is "on the black." Where does that expression come from and what does it refer to?

A Umpire historian Jim Evans puts it this way: "In the major leagues, home plate is of whitened rubber with a black, beveled border. The bevel is to prevent injury to a player sliding. The black is not technically part of the 17-inch plate. Technically, if a pitch is 'on the black, ' it is a ball."

Leaving behind a medical legacy

When Crestline, Ohio, named a baseball field for Gates Brown, I began to think about the most prestigious way to honor a player.

To have a field or ballpark named after you is great, but what about other tributes?

Players' names have been used for high schools, streets, racehorses, sandlot leagues and in many other ways.

The two top recognition honors are in the medical field — a disease and an operation. Who hasn't heard of Lou Gehrig's disease and the Tommy John operation?

Gehrig, slugger of the powerhouse Yankees, was the epitome of strength and manliness. In the midst of his career, an insidious ailment left him weak, unable to perform in the sport in which he excelled. The first announcement was that he had chronic infantile paralysis, which would never become worse. Then came an official diagnosis from the Mayo Clinic that the ailment was amyotrophic lateral sclerosis (ALS). Within three years, Gehrig was dead, but ALS lives on far beyond the boundaries of baseball as Lou Gehrig's disease.

Tommy John was less of a star than Gehrig. However, his career spanned 26 seasons and brought 288 victories. After starting with the

Indians, Tommy went to the White Sox where for two years, 1966-67, he led the league in shutouts. Traded to the Dodgers in 1972 for Dick Allen, he became more effective.

In 1973, he led the National League in winning percentage with a 16-9 record. The next season was beginning to look like his best. He was 13-3 when he suffered an injured left elbow in July.

Enter Dr. Frank Jobe with his now-famous Tommy John operation, a ligament transplant. This was a procedure never performed on a pitcher. Jobe estimated the odds of the 31-year-old left-hander pitching again at 100-1.

After the operation, John rehabilitated for a year and a half, rejoining the Dodgers in 1976. Eventually, he was better than ever. He pitched 14 years after the operation and racked up three seasons with more than 20 victories.

It was an outstanding career. Yet, John is more famous for lending his name to the Tommy John operation than for his pitching record.

Far removed from the renown of Gehrig and John is Harold Epps, a Cardinal prospect in the late 1930s. In a different way, he, too, lent his name to baseball's lexicon.

I heard about Epps from Branch Rickey when I went to Brooklyn in 1948 for my first major league job. When he bossed the Cardinals, Rickey had high hopes for Epps. However, the rookie outfielder ruined his promising career with his overenthusiastic pursuit of the ever-tempting pleasures of his lengthy honeymoon.

After Epps' example, Rickey and his followers forever had a name for the problem — "Eppsitis."

The word never accrued the fame of Lou Gehrig's disease or the Tommy John operation, but did earn a small place in the fine print of baseball lore.

ORIGINALLY PRINTED APRIL 26, 2009.

ASK ERNIE!

ERNIE HARWELL ANSWERS READERS' QUESTIONS

PURNAL GOLDY

Q How about Purnal Goldy, remember him? He was a fantastic fastball hitter and looked like the next Ted Williams. Then someone discovered he couldn't hit a curve, and he was soon gone. Any idea whatever happened to him?

A Purnal Goldy was a short-lived wonder. After a terrific buildup, he joined the Tigers in midseason of 1962. He played only 20 games and hit .229. He was back in 1963, but used only as a pinch-hitter with two hits in eight trips.

I couldn't find anyone to tell me about where he is now. I heard many years ago that he married a rich lady from Denver and his lifestyle kept him from worrying about being a big-league flop. Incidentally, Goldy, who stretched out to 6-feet-5, was one of the tallest Tigers of all time. Tony Clark stands the tallest at 6-8.

Cupped bat has history of success

Despite the long-established wisdom that pitching and defense win pennants, talk about the 2008 Tigers will focus on bats.

There's no doubting the power of manager Jim Leyland's batting order. There are no rest stops in an opposing pitcher's trip through the Tigers' starting lineup.

So, this is about bats — a hitter's weapon. A bat to a ballplayer is like a rifle to a Marine.

My most cherished boyhood Christmas gift was a bat. Those were 1930 Depression days when a top-notch Louisville Slugger sold for $2, but my parents made a sacrifice to buy it for me. A current big league model sells for more than $70.

I've heard stories of players taking favorite bats to bed, Babe Ruth ordering 54-ounce bats, Ty Cobb using a bat that weighed 44 ounces, and Hillerich & Bradsby — the company that makes Louisville Sluggers — allowing one player to select his own wood: Ted Williams.

My favorite bat story concerns Lou Brock and the cupped bat, now used by many major leaguers.

After the 1968 World Series against the Tigers, Brock visited Japan with the St. Louis Cardinals. He watched in awe as Sadaharu Oh hit tremendous home runs and asked him for one of his bats. He

JULIAN H. GONZALEZ

Like many modern players, Detroit's Carlos Guillen uses ash and maple bats. He might use four different bats in the same game.

discovered it was different — cupped at the end where the wood had been hollowed out for better balance.

Brock began using the new bat the following season and was still using it when he got his 3,000th career hit Aug. 13, 1979. He was the first to use the cupped bat in the big leagues.

The story has an ironic twist. Researchers discovered the bat originated in America and was copied by the Japanese.

In 1910, the Savannah Bat Co. introduced the Tea Cup bat, identical to today's cupped model. It attracted little attention at the time. But the Japanese discovered it and used it to design their version.

Nobody knows who invented the Tea Cup, but here's a thought. In 1910, Cobb was at the peak of his career with the Tigers. His hometown of Royston is not far from Savannah, Ga.

Could it have been ol' Tyrus who started the trend?

ORIGINALLY PRINTED MARCH 30, 2008.

ASK ERNIE!

ERNIE HARWELL ANSWERS READERS' QUESTIONS

RANKING CURTIS GRANDERSON

Q I believe that Curtis Granderson is among the premier centerfielders in the game today. Where does he rank in your book?

A I've watched some great Tigers centerfielders — Mickey Stanley, Chet Lemon, Gary Peters — but Granderson is the best. My all-time picks would be Willie Mays, Mickey Mantle, Joe DiMaggio and Tris Speaker. Among current players, I'd select Ken Griffey Jr., Torii Hunter and Granderson as tops. Right now, Hunter might be a shade better than Granderson.

HITTING STREAKS

Q Has a hitter ever extended his hitting streak by coming to the plate but having no official time at bat? What if he walked or sacrificed at each plate appearance? Would his consecutive-game hitting streak still be alive?

A The rule is the same for a hitting streak and for a consecutive-game hitting streak. They cannot be terminated by a walk, hit batter or a sacrifice bunt. A sac fly can end the streak. So, many hitters' streaks have been helped by this regulation.

Just a dash of pepper can be spicy

The old-time game of "pepper" may be making a comeback. Once an integral part of pregame practice, it faded away some 20 years ago, but the Seattle Mariners are reviving it.

Pepper was a great exercise. A batter would face several fielders lined up 20 feet away. He would hit the ball directly at the players, and they would have to react quickly. It was good training for the batter. And the fielders also improved their skills.

I remember newsreels of the St. Louis Cardinals playing pepper before their 1934 World Series games against the Tigers. The Cards were acrobatic, adding all kinds of tricks and gimmicks to their games. Fans loved to watch. And the players also seemed to derive a lot of enjoyment.

Why did pepper disappear? The main reason is that ballclubs began to schedule such structured practice regimes before their games that there was hardly time left to squeeze in a game of pepper. Also, the modern players now can relax before each game in a luxurious clubhouse with their own café — something more tempting than another kind of pregame exercise.

There are other reasons. Groundskeepers are stricter now and more eager to protect their turf. Pepper players often would hit balls into the stands, and safety-conscious executives began to frown on the game.

Seattle players are trying to bring back the wonderful game of pepper. They are playing it again before every game. Let's hope the comeback will last.

Like pepper, there are others parts of the game I miss. Don't get me wrong. The players of today are super-skilled and better coached. The diamonds are better kept and fans' accommodations much improved. Baseball has survived a lot of bad things off the field. I truly believe that the game as it is played between the lines today is just as good and exciting as ever.

Still, I rue that, over the years, technical progress has erased many colorful sidelights. Here are some of them: Ladies Day ... many fans keeping score of each game ... bleachers ... knot-hole gangs ... long train rides with the teams ... typewriters in the press box and Western Union operators to work with the writers ... re-created broadcasts ... the newspaper extra editions for sports events ... afternoon World Series games ... and — even more recent — whatever happened to the game-winning RBI as a stat?

ORIGINALLY PRINTED AUGUST 30, 2009.

ERNIE HARWELL

ASK ERNIE!

ERNIE HARWELL ANSWERS READERS' QUESTIONS

GAMES AFTER ALL-STAR GAME

Q I say there have been Major League Baseball games played on Wednesday, the day after the All-Star Game. Am I correct?

A You are correct. Tim Wiles at the Baseball Hall of Fame confirms that the last game played on a Wednesday after the All-Star Game was July 11, 1995. A players' strike that season forced the change. Six games were played on that date.

LADIES DAY

Q Do you remember Ladies Day at Navin Field?

A I wasn't in Detroit in those days, but I certainly remember Ladies Days. The custom began in 1867. In the late 1880s, Cincinnati staged a Ladies Day every afternoon the suave and handsome Tony Mullane was scheduled to pitch. The event came to a halt in the 1970s when court rulings and political correctness decided it discriminated against male fans.

OUT OF LEFTFIELD

ERNIE ON THE MIKE:

They're having a confab at the mound.

WHEN THE PITCHER, CATCHER AND MANAGER MEET ON THE MOUND MID-INNING

Lohrke was truly 'Lucky' off the field

The notice of former major leaguer Jack Lohrke's death was relegated to the obscurity of fine print. Yet, in his time — the 1940s and early '50s — he was famous, not as a player, but as an example of Lefty Gomez's oft-quoted saying, "I'd rather be lucky than good."

His nickname was "Lucky." And if anybody ever rightly earned his nickname, it was Lohrke. Jack didn't like that tag, possibly because he didn't gain it on the playing field. It was the result of his three escapes from death before he even reached the major leagues.

His first stroke of good fortune came during his World War II Army career, when he fought in the D-Day invasion of Normandy and the Battle of the Bulge. Once, four soldiers — two on each side of him — were killed in battle, but he was spared.

After the war, Jack was scheduled to fly home to California on a military transport plane. He was bumped from the flight and his seat given to a high-ranking officer. All passengers on that plane died in a crash.

Lohrke's good luck followed him from the military into baseball. In 1946, Jack was riding on the bus with his Spokane teammates. When the players got off for a lunch stop, he was informed of his pro-

motion to San Diego, then a Triple-A team. He
grabbed his baggage and hitchhiked home. The
team bus he left ran off a mountain road and
crashed. Nine of Jack's Spokane teammates were
killed.

Lohrke broke into the majors with the New York
Giants in 1947. On Sept. 1 of his rookie season, he
hit a home run in the first game of a doubleheader.
It was the Giants' 183rd homer of the season,
breaking the record held by the 1936 Yankees.
Lohrke added another home run in the second
game.

He played third base in 112 games that year, but
he never hit the 100-game mark in any of his next
six seasons. Jack pinch-hit for the Giants in the 1951
World Series, going 0-for-2. After five years with
the Giants, he finished his career with the Phils in
1952 and '53.

A personal note: When Lohrke was with the
Giants, I broadcast his games in 1950 and 1951. Our
sponsor for all games on both radio and TV was
Chesterfield cigarettes. The company's biggest
competitor was the American Tobacco Co. whose
product, Lucky Strike, was usually called "Luckies."

Whenever Jack Lohrke was involved in a play,
Chesterfield would not allow Russ Hodges and me
to mention his famous nickname.

He was Lucky, but we were Chesterfield.

ORIGINALLY PRINTED MAY 24, 2009.

ASK ERNIE!

ERNIE HARWELL ANSWERS READERS' QUESTIONS

KNUCKLEBALL PITCHERS

Q All the knuckleball pitchers in major leagues seem to be right-handed. Have there ever been any left-handed knuckleball pitchers?

A Left-handed knucklers are scarce. But the first knuckler ever was a left-hander. He was Thomas H. (Toad) Ramsey, who pitched for Louisville in the American Association (then a major league) in the mid-1880s. Toad struck out 499 batters in 1886 (second all-time high) and won 38 games.

He turned to the knuckle ball when, as an apprentice bricklayer, he lost his middle finger after a load of bricks fell on him.

Probably the best known left-handed knuckleball pitcher was Wilbur Wood. After brief stints with Boston and Pittsburgh, he joined the White Sox in 1967 and pitched for them for 12 years. He never threw the trick pitch until he reached the majors.

Another left-handed knuckler was Mickey Haefner, who was on the Washington Senators' staff in 1945 with three other pitchers who also threw the butterfly pitch — Roger Wolff, Dutch Leonard and Johnny Niggeling.

Goofy trades not new in baseball

Here's an item to put on the goofy baseball trades list.

In 2008, the Calgary Vipers swapped pitcher John Odom to a Laredo, Texas, team for 10 baseball bats.

The Tigers made this list in 1905. Detroit owed spring training rent to Augusta, Ga. The Tigers paid the debt by leaving pitcher Ed Cicotte (later a star with the Chicago Black Sox) with the Augusta team.

The St. Louis Browns pulled the same kind of deal in 1913, leaving Buzzy Wares with the Montgomery, Ala., team for spring training rental.

Another player was exchanged for a fence. He was Hall of Famer Lefty Grove, then with Martinsburg, W. Va. Baltimore Orioles owner Jack Dunn discovered that Martinsburg owed money for construction of an outfield fence. He offered to pay the debt, and Martinsburg let the Orioles take Grove in exchange.

Hunger caused some of the strangest trades.

Wichita Falls, Texas, traded Euel Moore for a plate of beans. Dallas sent Joe Martina to New Orleans for two barrels of oysters. Hence, the pitcher's nickname, "Oyster Joe." And San Francisco shipped Jack Fenton to Memphis for a box of prunes.

My favorite food trade was pulled off by the irrepressible Joe Engel, president of the Chattanooga Lookouts. In 1931, Joe swapped his shortstop, Johnny Jones, to Charlotte, N.C., for a Thanksgiving turkey. He then served the turkey to the writers who covered his team.

Even Cy Young, baseball's winningest pitcher, made the goofy trades list. Young was so lightly regarded as a rookie that his first team — Canton, Ohio — peddled him to Cleveland for a suit of clothes. In those days, a suit probably cost no more than $10.

Speaking of money, here's the topper.

Willis Hudlin made the cleverest trade of all. He retired in 1940 after pitching 15 years in the big leagues — every season but one with the Cleveland Indians. He then became a pitcher and part-owner of the Little Rock Travelers in the Southern League. In 1944, owner Hudlin traded pitcher Hudlin to the St. Louis Browns. He pitched only two innings for the Browns and had an 0-1 record. But the Browns won the pennant that season, and Hudlin received a World Series share. That winter, owner Hudlin of Little Rock bought back pitcher Hudlin from the Browns and kept the change.

There's one more goofy trade. In 1948, the Brooklyn Dodgers sent their Montreal catcher, Cliff Dapper, to the Atlanta Crackers for the Atlanta announcer. His name is on the cover of this book.

ORIGINALLY PRINTED JUNE 2, 2008.

ASK ERNIE!

ERNIE HARWELL ANSWERS READERS' QUESTIONS

1950 TIGERS

Q Very little has been written about the Tiger team of 1950. I believe it was one of the finest. The three outfielders averaged over .300. George Kell, my favorite, hit over .300. Shortstop Johnny Lipon and second baseman Gerry Priddy were good hitters, too.

A That team almost won the pennant, finishing second, three games behind the Yankees. Many fans blame their loss on "Robinson's Rock." Aaron Robinson, who had come to Detroit the year before in the worst deal in Tigers history, failed to tag Cleveland's Bob Lemon at the plate in a crucial late-season game. Robinson, traded to the Tigers by the White Sox for Billy Pierce, had two and a half mediocre years here. After only 27 games for Detroit, Pierce crafted a brilliant 16-year career with the White Sox and San Francisco.

ASK ERNIE!

ERNIE HARWELL ANSWERS READERS' QUESTIONS

THE GREATEST GAME EVER?

Q The most exciting game I've ever seen was the Tigers' 10-9 win over the Yankees in 1950 at Briggs Stadium. Could you give me details?

A Many fans agree. Super Tiger fan Max Lapides put this one on his favorite list in a Free Press Magazine article, Aug. 13, 1967. He capsuled it this way: "June 23, 1950. Record set with 11 home runs for the two teams. Tigers won in the ninth on a two-run, inside-the-park home run by Hoot Evers. All runs were scored as direct result of home runs."

The Yankees jumped to a 6-0 lead, but the Tigers overtook them with an eight-run outburst, featuring a grand slam by pitcher Dizzy Trout. The long-ball battle reached a climax in the ninth. Tom Henrich hit a two-run blast to give New York a 9-8 lead, but Evers topped him with his dramatic blow.

Lapides captured the moment: "With coach Dick Bartell frantically waving him on, Evers swept around third just as DiMaggio made the only bad play I ever saw him make. His hard throw to Rizzuto was wide — pulling him off balance and ruining any chance he had to catch Evers. It was an inside-the-park home run. ... The Tigers had won, 10-9, to climax the greatest slugfest in Tiger history."

The origins of some familiar terms

As Tigers broadcasters, my partners and I received a lot of mail. Some of it was kind. The rest, we turned over to the FBI.

There were all kinds of suggestions. The most popular involved the microphone and where we could jam it — a physical impossibility. I took a lot of kidding about my interest in baseball history, especially references to the origin of baseball terms.

For instance, how did "charley horse" and "bullpen" get started?

"Charley horse" entered baseball's lexicon this way. Pop Anson's Chicago White Stockings in the mid-1880s took a day off from their schedule to visit the racetrack. Several players bet on a horse named Charley, which pulled up lame in the stretch and lost.

The next day, in pregame practice, one of the White Sox players suffered a leg cramp and began to limp.

"Hey," said one of his unsympathetic teammates. "Look at him. Just like that horse Charley. He's got a Charley Horse."

The term "bullpen" has a couple of explanations about its beginning. One is that the term started because the pitchers warmed up under the Bull

Durham tobacco sign. (There seemed to be one in every baseball park in America.)

Another is that it came from the cattlemen out West. The pitchers who were called into the game for relief duty were compared to bulls being brought in for slaughter. Thus, the place they came from was called the bullpen.

You can take your choice of those versions.

Then there's the old expression, "Hooray for our side."

This goes back to Lady Godiva. Remember, she rode through the streets of Coventry, England, in protest of high taxes. She not only rode bareback — in the true sense of the word — but she rode sidesaddle, attracting a large crowd of men who jammed the sidewalks for a good look.

As Lady Godiva rode down the street, an enthusiastic looker on the side she faced yelled out for all to hear, "Hooray for our side."

Yes, it's strange, isn't it, how baseball terms originated?

ORIGINALLY PRINTED APRIL 21, 2008.

ASK ERNIE!

ERNIE HARWELL ANSWERS READERS' QUESTIONS

TIGERS' HOUSE BAND

Q Was there ever a "house band" that played at Tiger games? I believe the Dodgers in Brooklyn had some type of band that played during their games. If there was this type of musical group, did they have some type of theme songs?

A The Tigers did have a house band — a very good one. The leader was Merle Alvey, who was president of the Detroit Federation of Musicians, Local 5 from 1966 to 1985. Merle also led the Tiger Dixieland Band that moved through the stands to entertain the fans up close. The big band made it to the New York Times front page during the 1968 World Series. A photo of Jose Feliciano singing the national anthem prior to Game 5 showed Merle and the boys in the background.

You are right about the Dodgers. At Ebbets Field, the Dodger Symphony fractured music during every game. Several Brooklyn fans with no musical talent or experience would toot the strike-out victim of the opposing team back to his dugout with a loud refrain of "umpty-do, umpty–do."

Mick's long single one for the books

T housands of words have been written about baseball's longest home run. But what about the longest single?

This overlooked historical moment happened at Yankee Stadium on Aug. 10, 1956.

Here's how Joe Sheehan of the New York Times reported it:

"Mickey Mantle came through with a big ninth-inning wallop off Billy Loes to give the Yankees a 5-4 decision over the Orioles at the stadium last night.

"With Billy Martin on third and two out, Mantle hit a towering 450-foot drive to center. The ball landed on the running track and bounced some 15 feet up into the centerfield bleachers for a ground-rule double."

I know. You're saying, "Isn't the topic of this column supposed to be the longest single? Now, you're writing about a double."

Explanation: It was a double, at least for a while. But it was changed to a single, in accordance with the scoring rules.

I broadcast that game for the Orioles. And for years, my memory prompted me to tell everybody that I first called the hit a double, but before signing off, I reported that the official scorer had

1966 FILE PHOTO

Yankees great Mickey Mantle finished his career with 2,415 hits, but a long single in 1956 recorded as a double is still in dispute.

changed his ruling to a single.

Yet, Sheehan in the Times wrote that it was Mantle's second double of the game. The Sporting News issue of Aug. 22 — 12 days after the game — said the same thing in its review and box score.

In my effort to verify my memory of the hit as a

single, I encountered a few surprises. Ken Hirdt at Elias Sports Bureau, the official statistician of Major League Baseball, located the game and the precise date. His check of the official scorer's report showed a double and a single for Mantle, not two doubles.

Ken's info was confirmed by Dave Smith of Retrosheet. Dave sent me the game's play-by-play and photo copies of the Yankees and Orioles scorebooks. These proved that Mantle's first double came in the third inning, in which the Yankees failed to score. That meant his one RBI came on the ninth-inning hit and had to be a single. Also, the official play-by-play of that final inning said: "Mantle singled to centerfield and Martin scored."

The Yankees scorekeeper also noted in his ninth-inning entry that Mantle's hit "bounced once into cf bleachers."

There is no doubt the hit was a single. Yet, my fellow researchers and I have never been able to find a correction of the original story. In printed material, it is always a double.

But now, all of us have the proof.

It was not a double. Mantle's game-winning hit was a 465-foot single, the longest in baseball history.

ORIGINALLY PRINTED APRIL 14, 2008.

100

ASK ERNIE!

ERNIE HARWELL ANSWERS READERS' QUESTIONS

TURNED DOWN INTERVIEWS

Q **Over the years, what players turned you down for an interview?**

A Sometimes a starting pitcher wouldn't like to do an interview. However, almost every other player was willing. One starter I remember turning me down was one of my best friends in baseball, Tommy John, then with the White Sox.

Another friend, Mickey Mantle, had what I thought was a strange reaction. He was willing — almost eager — for me to interview him when he was a player. But later, when he was broadcasting Yankee games for a short time, he politely declined to go on the air with me.

Colored bats a no-no, but there's a gray area

Everybody is talking and writing about maple bats. Forget maple. What about red bats? I was under the impression that colored bats were illegal. But shortstop Edgar Renteria and others have been using them.

So, I checked with the official rule book.

Rule 1:10 says: "No colored bat may be used in a professional game unless approved by the Rules Committee."

To find out what colors had been approved, I contacted Russ Carlton, media coordinator of the Tigers, and Rick Vaughn, vice president of communications of the Tampa Bay Rays.

John McHale Jr., executive vice president of administration of the commissioner's office and former Tigers president, forwarded this explanation to Vaughn:

"Page two of bulletin C-3, issued by the commissioner to the umpires, describes approved bat colors as natural finish, brown wood stain, black and half-stain (Walker finish). Red is not an approved color and any bat that appears reddish probably started out to be stained brown. Any umpire has the authority to exclude a bat of unauthorized color from any game."

Carlton confirmed that a red bat was not permit-

JULIAN H. GONZALEZ

During his time with the Tigers, Edgar Renteria used a reddish brown bat. The bat must begin with a brown finish to be legal.

ted and agreed that any bat that seemed red likely had begun with a brown finish. Carlton added that umpires test a bat by checking its grain. If the grain shows through, the bat can be used.

The term "Walker finish" in the McHale explanation might have baffled you. It describes the two-tone bat that became popular in the early 1950s.

While visiting the Louisville Slugger factory, Harry Walker, one-time National League batting champion, saw a bat whose barrel had been in a vat of black varnish. He liked the two-toned aspect of the natural wood handle and the barrel darkened by the varnish.

Walker began to hit well with that bat and other hitters copied him. It became a popular model, still used by many players.

Next, my quest took me to American League umpire Rick Reed.

"What action do you take if a batter comes to the plate with a red bat or some other color not authorized?" I asked.

"I'd make him get another bat," Reed said. "There's no penalty in the rules. If, because of the umpire's or the opposing team's oversight, he hits a home run with the illegal bat, the play still stands and cannot be protested."

If the rule is that lenient, why do the rule makers even bother about a red bat or a bat of any color?

ORIGINALLY PRINTED AUGUST 18, 2008.

ASK ERNIE!

ERNIE HARWELL ANSWERS READERS' QUESTIONS

GLOVES ON FIELD

Q | I used to see Joe DiMaggio and others throw their gloves on the field at the end of an inning. How long did this go on before someone tripped over a glove?

A | This custom ended after the 1953 season. Strangely enough, no glove left on the field ever caused any significant problem with a ball in play. It did help create fun opportunities for practical jokers. Phil Rizzuto, who had a fearful aversion to rodents, once found a dead rat in his glove. And a prankster who often played Hearts with Johnny Pesky hid the dastardly Queen of Spades in Johnny's glove.

INSIDE THE GAME

66 **ERNIE ON THE MIKE:**

The Tigers need some instant runs. **99**

WHEN DETROIT FALLS BEHIND LATE IN A GAME

Today's superstars carry a heavy burden

D on't envy the modern baseball star. When fans look at the big bucks, the fancy lifestyle and personal perks of stardom, they wish they could achieve the same glorified status. But don't be too quick to dream of living like the rich superstar. There are many negatives that come with his much-envied territory.

I believe the star of today's baseball world has a tougher existence than his counterpart of the past. In the 1920s, '30s and '40s, big-league headliners existed in a simpler environment. TV had not burst upon the scene. There was no talk radio. Sports writers simply covered each game and did not consider themselves investigative reporters.

In those days, a few superstars were rich. But the average big leaguer augmented his salary with an off-season job. Today, even the most unnoticed utilityman can afford to use his off-season to advantage. He can rest, travel or spend time conditioning. Many of today's athletes build gyms and maintain a personal trainer. When they report for spring training, they are already in top condition. But the player of the past, after working all winter, needed spring training to whip himself into shape for the coming season.

There's no doubt the modern star maintains a

DAVID P. GILKEY

During his one season with the Tigers in 2000, Juan Gonzalez
had his lowest RBI total (67) in 10 years and hit just 22 homers.

lifestyle we all might want to strive for. But there
are negatives that loom large for today's baseball
player. Big money, public envy and intense media
attention have combined to put tremendous pressure on the big-time star. This is a pressure much

more severe than in the past.

Much of it began to develop with TV. In the past, a game was reported with a newspaper story and a box score. Now, TV and radio cover every game. Mistakes are magnified. Talk radio's overanalysis of every fault puts extra pressure on the player.

Like any celebrity of modern times, the baseball star is exposed to microscopic inspection. Not only do members of the media examine his play on the field, but they rake through his personal life as if he were a presidential candidate.

So, the life of a baseball star is reduced to two categories — perks or pressure. It's a great life — one to be envied — but it comes with a cost.

Take the case of Juan Gonzalez, the superstar the Tigers acquired from Texas to swing his big bat and charm the club's long-suffering fans. Juan had his own entourage — a trainer, personal business manager and spiritual adviser. They all traveled with the big star.

Gonzalez never fit the vastness of the new Comerica Park or the rest of the city. He hated Detroit and quickly moved on — a complete bust. His career never recovered, and he left baseball at a fairly early age.

Gonzalez enjoyed the perks. But the pressure did him wrong.

Yes, we can envy the big stars. But, remember, there is always a heavy personal cost for baseball celebrity.

ORIGINALLY PRINTED MAY 12, 2008.

ASK ERNIE!

ERNIE HARWELL ANSWERS READERS' QUESTIONS

JACK MORRIS

Q Can you give me a reason why Jack Morris has never made the Hall of Fame with his record, especially his World Series record?

A Some of the theories about Morris being overlooked are: He didn't play in the big eastern cities, which are centers of communication; Jack was edgy sometimes with the writers, who do the voting; and he didn't have the color or flamboyance, which is sometimes needed.

I contend that he belongs because he was the top winner and dominant pitcher in the '80s, he turned in brilliant performances on the big stage — the World Series — and his lifetime record compares favorably to many other pitchers who've been enshrined at Cooperstown.

Wild-card races spice September

The Lords of Baseball had it right when they adopted the wild card. In earlier years, the American League pennant chase was often a cruel joke because the Yankees were so far ahead that other teams were merely playing out their schedules. Now, with the wild card, several communities keep on running a baseball fever in September, regardless of how big a margin the division leaders boast.

Speaking of September and the Yankees: In mid-September 1928, the New Yorkers clinched the American League pennant in Detroit. Babe Ruth threw a big party for his teammates at the Book-Cadillac Hotel. He called room service for a piano. The hotel told the Babe it didn't have one. So, he went out and bought one. Nobody ever told me what the Babe did with that piano after the party was over.

Are today's fielders much better than they were 10 to 50 years ago? I think so. Today, sensational catches — especially by outfielders — happen with astounding regularity. The trademark play of this decade is the leap at the fence, changing a potential home run into a putout. I've never seen so many great catches. The modern glove is the reason. The giant size started in 1935 with Hank Greenberg and has become a standard. Also, for outfielders, the new stadiums provide better playing conditions. Most of the fences are padded and warning tracks help the outfielders gauge their approaches much better.

Have you noticed that major league careers are getting longer? The increase is because of a couple of factors. First, the big money is a real incentive to stick around an extra year or so — even if skills are starting to diminish. Second, most of today's players keep in better condition than their earlier counterparts. And with the larger salaries they can afford personal trainers or their own workout facilities.

A recent scientific study of almost 6,000 former big-league players found that the average length of a career was 5.6 years. From 1902 to 1945, the figure was 4.3.

ORIGINALLY PRINTED SEPTEMBER 10, 2007.

All-Star Game has lost some luster

T he All-Star Game started as merely a one-time adjunct to the 1933 Chicago World's Fair. At that time, most of the owners didn't favor its continuance. They wanted it for one time only.

Baseball's All-Star attraction is the best of all the sports. It's the only one that displays any true competition. Still, the modern baseball classic has lost some of its charm.

When the game started, watching players of the other league was a novelty. Now, an American League fan can watch National Leaguers via interleague play or by tuning in on TV to all the numerous major league games available each day.

Another factor that has dulled the brilliance of the game is free agency. Years ago, players didn't switch leagues so easily. Also, all the surrounding hoopla (the Home Run Derby, for instance) has taken much of the focus away from the game itself.

Broadcasting an All-Star Game is one of an announcer's toughest assignments. With so many distractions, the managers, coaches and players are difficult to reach. And the numerous lineup changes can certainly be a real challenge.

All-Star history is not without gaffes. One came in 1959, when it was decided to stage two All-Star Games each year. This happened because of the players' greed. Since their pension plan derived money from the All-Star gate receipts, they insisted on scheduling two games instead of one. The plan was a disaster. Two games reduced the event's drama and were difficult to work into the regular schedule. The powers that be got smart and returned to the one-game-a-year plan after the four-year mistake.

Another black mark in All-Star history was the 2002 game in Milwaukee. That's the one that ended in a 7-7 tie when the teams ran out of pitchers. I blame that fiasco on the pressure put on the managers to see that every All-Star selected gets into the game. I say, play it to win for your league. Use the players you need to win and forget the problem of everybody getting playing time.

ORIGINALLY PRINTED JULY 14, 2008.

ASK ERNIE!

ERNIE HARWELL ANSWERS READERS' QUESTIONS

LET'S PLAY TWO!

Q As a kid in Detroit, I remember two All-Star Games being played each year. Is my memory correct?

A Your memory is good. In the late 1950s, the players figured they could enhance their pension fund by playing two All-Star Games each year. They did this for four straight years. Here are the sites for those years: 1959: Pittsburgh and Los Angeles' Memorial Coliseum; 1960: K.C. and New York's Yankee Stadium; 1961: San Francisco and Boston; 1962: Washington and Chicago's Wrigley Field. The experiment didn't work. Two All-Star Games in one season turned out to be one too many. The regular-season schedule couldn't handle a double interruption.

Tidbits and trivia from game's past

Here's a glimpse into some curious items from baseball history:

◆ The game's most economical pitch count happened during World War II. On Aug. 10, 1944, Boston Braves right-hander Red Barrett threw only 58 pitches in his 2-0, nine-inning victory over Cincinnati. This is the same Red Barrett who was called "Red Barber" by Brooklyn PA man Tex Rickard. Apparently, Tex couldn't tell the difference between an incoming pitcher and a radio announcer.

◆ Only one major league team has ever gone through a complete season without being shut out. The New York Yankees did it in 1932. Their streak extended over two seasons, from Aug. 3, 1931, through Aug. 2, 1933.
How good were these world champions? They won 107 games and lost 47. They boasted nine Hall of Famers among the regulars: three of the four infielders (Lou Gehrig, Tony Lazzeri and Joe Sewell), two of the three outfielders (Babe Ruth and Earle Combs), three pitchers (Red Ruffing, Lefty Gomez and Herb Pennock) and catcher Bill Dickey.

◆ A reserve outfielder on that team was Sammy

Byrd, known as "Babe Ruth's legs." Sammy quit baseball for the pro golf tour in 1936. While head pro at Detroit's Plum Hollow he won the Michigan Open and Michigan PGA in 1944 and took the PGA again in 1945.

Sammy is the only man to play in both the World Series and the Masters. He was a defensive replacement for Ruth in the '32 Series, and he finished twice in the top 10 of the Masters — in 1941-42. In his last Masters appearance, Byrd shot a 10 on the second hole at Augusta, the highest ever on that hole.

◆ At 17, Bob Feller pitched in 1936 for the Cleveland Indians while he was on vacation from high school. When Bob graduated from Van Meter (Iowa) High School, NBC covered the event.

◆ Dazzy Vance, the great Brooklyn right-hander, refused to pitch when the Dodgers played the Philadelphia Phillies at Baker Bowl. "It might hurt my record," he said. Imagine a modern day major leaguer getting away with a statement like that?

◆ Weather note: For four straight days in 1945 (May 14 through May 17), every American League game was rained out. The Philadelphia Phillies were rained out 10 consecutive days in August 1909.

◆ Now, from our drought department, how's this? The entire White Sox team hit only three home runs in their 1909 schedule of 154 games. Homers

were hit by Bill Isbell, Fielder Jones and pitcher
Ed Walsh. That's a record for nonproduction in
the AL. The NL record for fewest homers is nine
by the 1917 Pirates.

ORIGINALLY PRINTED JUNE 7, 2009.

ASK ERNIE!

ERNIE HARWELL ANSWERS READERS' QUESTIONS

OLDE ENGLISH D

Q I'm sure I'm not the first to notice this. Why is the Olde English D on the Tigers' cap different from the D on their home jerseys?

A Some time ago, the change was made. Nobody seems to know when or why or by whom. Here is what Rick Thompson of the Tigers' PR office said: "This question began to surface often a few years ago. We did intense research. Even enlisted the help of Sharon Arend, director of archives and historical documents at Ilitch Holding Inc. No one could find the answer. It is still a mystery."

ASK ERNIE!

ERNIE HARWELL ANSWERS READERS' QUESTIONS

STEALING HOME

Q Vic Power stole home twice in one game in 1958. Were there any other players since 1930 who stole home twice in one game?

A On Aug. 14, 1958, Cleveland's Vic Power stole home twice to beat the Tigers, 10-9. The first steal came during a five-run rally in the eighth inning. After the Tigers scored two runs in the ninth to tie the game, Power won it for the Indians with a steal of home in the 10th, just beating Frank Lary's pitch to catcher Charlie Lau. This was the first time a player had stolen home twice in one game since Doc Gautreau of the Boston Braves did it in 1927. And nobody has done it since Power's accomplishment in 1958. Which means it has happened only twice in 82 years. Certainly a rare feat.

Baseball gimmicks: Fair and foul

Tampa Bay matched its magical 2008 season with a top-notch promotion. When a home run is hit by a Rays player, the fan takes the ball to the Fan Assistance Center. He or she waits while a team representative visits the clubhouse, gets the hitter's autograph on the ball and returns it to the fan.

Another inventive promotion happened in Baltimore in 2008. With the Orioles on a streak of losing every Sunday, the club's gimmick offered fans attending a Sunday game a free ticket ... if the Birds broke their losing streak that afternoon. The Orioles again lost that Sunday. Several Sundays later, the offer was increased to two free tickets. Again, Baltimore lost — this time to the Tigers. After that, the gimmick was abandoned.

Let's just say it started out as a given — direct from the NFL's "on any given Sunday" playbook. But it wasn't a given after all.

Some other quick hits:

◆ About baseball instant replay. I applaud the quest for accuracy, but have bad vibes about removing the human element of umpire error. The length of games will increase if the replay process last longer than an argument about the call.

◆ A new great book is "Baseball's Greatest Hit: The Story of Take Me Out to the Ball Game." It's a lavish, beautifully crafted tribute to baseball's anthem. Tim Wiles, director of research at the Baseball Hall of Fame, is one of the authors. The others are Andy Strasberg and Robert Thompson.

The song is America's third-most frequently sung tune. And it took Jack Norworth only 30 minutes to write the classic lyric. In the foreword, singer Carly Simon writes she often sat in the Brooklyn dugout during Dodger home games.

◆ Here are a couple of ironies from present-day baseball. Players are bigger, stronger and better conditioned; yet there are more injuries and more players on the disabled list. Players have advantage of more detailed instruction in colleges and the minor leagues. They study replays and detailed scouting reports; yet they don't execute the fundamentals of the game like players of the past.

◆ The record number for representatives from one club among the American League's top-10 hitters is three. The Toronto Blue Jays in 1993 had batting champion John Olerud finish at .363, followed by teammates Paul Molitor (.332) and Roberto Alomar (.326).

The National League goes back to 1893 for its batting trifecta. Three Phillies topped the list: Billy Hamilton (.380), Sam Thompson (.370) and

Ed Delahanty (.368).
Thompson is the Hall of Fame Tiger the Hall lists as a left-handed thrower, despite family proof that he threw right-handed.

ORIGINALLY PRINTED SEPTEMBER 1, 2008.

ASK ERNIE!

ERNIE HARWELL ANSWERS READERS' QUESTIONS

BEST STEALS OF HOME

Q What are some of the best steals of home that you witnessed?

A Two steals of home are burned into my memory. Jackie Robinson stole home in the first inning of the first major league game I broadcast. It was at Ebbets Field, Brooklyn, Aug. 4, 1948. Russ (Monk) Meyer was pitching for the Cubs. Jackie danced off third and raced home. He was safe on a very close play. The call by umpire Frank Dascoli sent Meyer into a rage. He raced toward the umpire and began to curse him. Dascoli ejected Meyer from the game. Russ' dirty words came over on our broadcast and the Cub pitcher was later fined and suspended.

The other steal of home came at Anaheim, Aug. 30, 1976. Dave Collins of the Angels did it against the Tigers. Tiger manager Ralph Houk charged from the dugout, protesting umpire Rich Garcia's call. On the radio I tried to say that catcher Bill Freehan "was beating his mitt at home plate." But the word "mitt," to my embarrassment, somehow came out another way.

NAMES TO KNOW

" **ERNIE ON THE MIKE:**

He has decided to ride the rapids with the incumbent. **"**

ON A MANGER ALLOWING THE PITCHER TO WORK OUT OF A JAM

Willard Brown hit historic HR in '47

You never know where you'll find a story — especially one that answers a tough trivia question. And the answer might even win you a few bucks at your favorite watering hole.

Before I get any deeper into the story, let me pose the question. Who was the first African American to hit a home run in the American League? Most folks are going to say Larry Doby. That is a logical answer, but it's wrong.

Doby became the first African American in the American League when Bill Veeck signed him to a Cleveland contract in July 1947. By that time, Jackie Robinson was the first African American to hit a home run in the National League. Robinson homered off Giants left-hander Dave Koslo at the Polo Grounds on April 18. It was Jackie's fourth big-league game.

Doby's prowess was home-run ability. But in his first season he played only 29 games — mostly as a pinch-hitter. And he did not connect for a home run.

However, the first homer by an African American in the AL did come that same season, 1947.

Soon after the Indians had signed Doby, the St. Louis Browns signed two players from the Kansas

City Monarchs of the Negro American League.
They were Hank Thompson and Willard Brown.
Each of the newcomers got into several games, but
without distinction.

For a brief time, though, Brown caught fire. Walt
Wilson, a veteran researcher, talked about it in the
Society for American Baseball Research's National
Pastime magazine, May 2004 issue.

"On July 23, Brown came up with four singles
and three RBI at Yankee Stadium and the Browns
beat New York, 8-2. Two days later he pounded out
two doubles against the Red Sox, but by early
August, Willard was back on the bench."

Then came the moment I want to target.

The Browns were hosting the Tigers in a twilight
doubleheader Aug. 13. The Tigers won the first
game, 7-1, and were leading the second, 5-4, in the
bottom of the eighth. There were only a few fans
left from the slim crowd of 3,002 when Willard
Brown pinch-hit against Hal Newhouser.

Brown swung and hit a drive deep to centerfield,
over the head of Hoot Evers. Brown raced around
the bases for an inside-the-park home run, the first
home run hit in the American League by an
African American.

It's the answer to that trivia question, and incidentally, it beat the Tigers, 6-5.

ORIGINALLY PRINTED SEPTEMBER 27, 2009.

ASK ERNIE!

ERNIE HARWELL ANSWERS READERS' QUESTIONS

OPENING DAY

 The Tigers' home opener is an unofficial holiday in Michigan. Workers fake coughs and call in sick. Tickets sell out. Children skip school. But has it always been that way?

 It probably goes back to the 1930s. Here in Detroit and in Cincinnati, those are the two places where Opening Day is an event. In other cities, sometimes it's ho-hum, sometimes it's a big event.

But in Cincinnati, they always used to have the honor of being the first game of the season. And in Detroit, it was a tradition, too. It was also big in Washington because the president threw out the first pitch, but that tradition ended, taking some shine off that game.

It's like Easter because you never know when it will be. Like Fourth of July because there's always some fireworks. And it's like Christmas because it's our time to open our new gift of baseball for the year.

Litwhiler pushed for pitcher's speed

t started in September 1974, with a photograph in the Michigan State student newspaper, The State News. Today, the radar gun to measure pitching speed is — for better or for worse — an integral part of the game.

MSU baseball coach Danny Litwhiler conceived the idea after seeing a picture of a campus cop with a device to catch speeders. Over the years, Danny built a reputation as the Thomas Edison of baseball with his many original ideas and inventions. He saw this as another project — the first accurate method to check baseball velocity.

Litwhiler recalls the gun's origin in his book, "Living the Baseball Dream."

"I knew the commander of the campus police, Adam Zutaut," he said. "I called him and asked if the gun could check the speed of a baseball. He said he didn't know, but would find out. Soon, he was at our baseball field. I had a catcher and two pitchers, a right-hander and a left-hander, waiting."

Litwhiler and Zutaut found that, in a primitive way, the gun was capable of measuring the speed of a pitch. Danny began his fine-tuning with the goal of producing a prototype.

His next move was to contact baseball commissioner Bowie Kuhn. "I told him that I didn't want

GABRIEL B. TAIT

The radar gun got its start in baseball when Michigan State coach Danny Litwhiler had the idea that it could measure pitch speeds.

any one club to have the gun, but hoped that all professional and amateur teams would use it," Danny said.

Kuhn notified the pro teams and within a week or two, Danny received phone calls, letters and telegrams asking about his new idea.

Litwhiler next approached his friend, John Paulson, developer of the JUGS pitching machine, to ask him if he could produce the speed gun. Paulson quickly developed a prototype.

In 1975, Litwhiler took the prototype to the Orioles' spring training camp in Miami. He showed it to manager Earl Weaver, who was immediately enthusiastic about the idea. Next, he displayed the gun to Cardinals manager Red Schoendienst, who became another convert.

Soon, Danny's invention became standard equipment for managers, scouts, and college and pro teams all over the world. It proved to be the first true way to measure the speed of a pitch. Today, no baseball man can do without it.

ORIGINALLY PRINTED JUNE 30, 2008.

ASK ERNIE!

ERNIE HARWELL ANSWERS READERS' QUESTIONS

1961 TIGERS

Q My favorite Tigers team did not win anything. But in 1961, they were 101-61. It was a great team! What are your thoughts of that ballclub under the great Bob Scheffing?

A That team was one of my favorites, too. It gave the great '61 Yankees a close battle until Labor Day. The Tigers went into a three-game series at Yankee Stadium only a game and a half behind the league-leading New Yorkers. Interest in Michigan for the Friday night opener was so intense that the Lions postponed their preseason football game until the following Monday.

The Tigers lost a heartbreaker in that first game when Whitey Ford outdueled Don Mossi, 1-0. The Yankees swept the series, and within a week, the race was over.

The Yankees finished with 109 victories, eight games ahead of Detroit. Third-place Baltimore was 14 games off the pace. K C and Washington tied for last place, each team 47.5 games behind the Yanks.

It was in 1961 that Roger Maris hit 61 homers to beat Babe Ruth's record. Norman Cash led the AL with a .361 average. The Tigers' top pitcher was Frank Lary with 23 victories.

Dalkowski was the true 'Wild Thing'

When I was broadcasting in Baltimore in 1957, I began to hear stories about Steve Dalkowski, a pitching phenom in the Orioles' farm system.

Dalkowski was a stocky, little left-hander (5-feet-10, 170 pounds) who didn't look like your usual hot-shot prospect. He wore glasses as thick as the bottom of a Coke bottle. But he could throw harder than anybody in baseball history.

Yet Dalkowski never reached the major leagues. His walk and wild-pitch totals exceeded his strike-outs. He was the phenom who failed.

My memory of Dalkowski is watching Orioles pitching coach Harry Brecheen trying to harness the youngster's wildness. I saw Steve in the bullpen, throwing his 110 m.p.h. pitch into the dirt or over the catcher's head. Manager Paul Richards — who made Dalkowski his special project — assigned an extra player to back up the catcher whenever Dalkowski warmed up. Brecheen, Richards and all others who tried could never cure his wildness.

In 1963, after eight years in the minors, Steve almost reached the majors. Orioles manager Billy Hitchcock told him he had made the club at the end of spring training. Steve was even fitted for a major league uniform. But that afternoon, pitching in relief against the Yankees, Dalkowski injured his left elbow. Never recovering from his injury, he had missed his big chance. After one more year, Baltimore released him and he wandered into obscurity.

Yet, whenever fast pitchers are discussed, Steve Dalkowski heads the list. Ted Williams faced him once in spring training. "He is the fastest ever," Ted said. "I never want to face him again."

In his nine-year minor league career, Steve was 46-80. He fanned 1,396 batters and walked 1,354 in 995 innings.

A normal game for Steve was seven innings, 18 strikeouts and 15 walks.

Here are some remarkable Dalkowski feats:

◆ Threw a no-hitter, walking 18 and striking out 20.

◆ Tore off a batter's ear with a wild pitch.

◆ Broke the mask of home-plate umpire Doug Harvey in three places.

◆ Threw a ball through a wooden fence.

◆ Hit a batter in the on-deck circle.

◆ Heaved a ball from deep centerfield over the press box.

◆ Made six consecutive wild pitches.

◆ Used 283 pitches in a complete game.

◆ Left a game after 120 pitches in two innings.

After Dalkowski departed from baseball, he was a lost soul.

Because of a drinking addiction he couldn't hold a job. He became a migrant farm laborer for almost 30 years. His health failed and was eventually diagnosed with dementia.

The last I heard, he was living in a nursing home in New Britain, Conn.

Like his pitches, Dalkowski's life was wild and uncontrollable. Although, he never pitched a major league game, his reputation reached the movies. Writer-director Ron Shelton, who also played in the Orioles' farm system, modeled the unpredictable Nuke LaLoosh in "Bull Durham" after Dalkowski.

ORIGINALLY PRINTED MAY 19, 2008.

ASK ERNIE!

ERNIE HARWELL ANSWERS READERS' QUESTIONS

BASEBALL RULES

Q Please give me a ruling on this play: Bases loaded, pitcher called for balk, but batter hits the pitch for single and two runs score. Should it be one run on the balk or does the play stand?

A Since the ball remained in play, the balk is nullified and the two runs score on the batter's single. Before 1956, the ball was ruled dead at the time of a balk, and no following action was acknowledged. This is still the rule used in high school baseball today.

Incidentally, at the winter meetings in 1956, American League president Will Harridge suggested that umpires signal a balk by dropping a handkerchief. His suggestion was immediately rejected.

Reed back in majors after health issues

Rochester's Rick Reed is the consummate umpire.

From the age of 13 when he called Little League balls and strikes for $5 per game to his 27th year in the major leagues, umpiring has been his passion. When Kevin Costner cast the role of the plate umpire in his movie "For Love of the Game" he chose Reed.

Take a moment to picture yourself stilling your passion for a year — not being able to work at the job you have loved and excelled in for a whole lifetime. That's what Reed suffered through in 2008.

But now, after a yearlong layoff because of poor health, Reed will be umpiring again. After two strokes, hundreds of doctors' visits and a grueling rehab, the veteran crew chief is back.

Rick had not umpired since May 27, 2008. He suffered a stroke the previous weekend in Denver, but worked through it during a Mets-Rockies game. He then flew home with 16-year-old son Tyler. While attending his aunt's funeral, he felt weak, and his speech seemed slurred, but he was determined to keep his next assignment in Milwaukee, where the Brewers were hosting Atlanta.

Disturbing symptoms continued to haunt him during the game. He was dizzy and felt off-balance

KIRTHMON F. DOZIER

Michigan native Rick Reed, a veteran umpire, is back on the job in the major leagues after two strokes and taking a year off.

when he ran. His crew insisted that the Milwaukee trainers treat him. They rushed Rick to the hospital, where it was determined he had suffered a blocked artery.

He was sent home to Rochester, Mich., to begin a long rehabilitation. He worked to get himself in shape for a comeback in 2009. All was going well until he suffered another stroke in February — just before spring training.

Dr. Michael Workings, Dr. Andrew Russman and the staff at Henry Ford Medical Center worked tirelessly with Rick. In March, he flew to Phoenix for an examination by the major leagues' appointed doctor.

"We cannot allow you to return to umpiring," Dr. Stephen Erickson told Rick. "Your health is not good enough to withstand the travel, lifestyle and other pressures of umpiring."

Rick was devastated by this official verdict. But he was determined not to give up. He challenged the ruling. And, with the support of his own doctors, he battled to return.

Finally, Rick was granted permission to work again. He was overjoyed when he received the phone call from Mark Letendre, director of Umpire Medical Services.

"What a thrill to get back," Rick said. "There were times when I had my doubts it would ever happen.

"I could not have made it without the support of my wonderful doctors and my wife, Cynthia. She and I have been married 32 years. Thirty of those, I've been an umpire. I really got to know her during those months at home. I learned to shop, cook, drive my son to school, take the dog to the vet and all those things that Mr. Mom has to do."

Now, despite two strokes and the pain and frustration of a lost year, he is ready once again to umpire in the major leagues.

ORIGINALLY PRINTED MAY 10, 2009.

ASK ERNIE!

ERNIE HARWELL ANSWERS READERS' QUESTIONS

SAC FLY RULE

Q My question concerns the sac fly rule. You stated it was eliminated in 1931, but was restored in 1939 and survived the 1954 changes. I have read that if there would have been a sac fly in 1941 when Ted Williams hit .406, he would have batted at least seven points higher. Was there a sac fly rule in effect for the 1941 season?

A You are right about the rule. It was restored in 1939, but in 1940 it was rescinded. So, Williams got no benefit from the rule when he batted .406 in 1941. At that time, the sacrifice fly was charged as a time at-bat. In 1954 the rule was restored to take away the time at-bat.

Yanks' bench coach has Tigers roots

A former Tigers farmhand is a key figure in the Yankees dugout. He is bench coach Rob Thomson, who knows more about the Tigers than any other Yankee.

Thomson's specialized, spy-like talent stems from his experience with the Yankees as a field coordinator and video expert. Beginning in 2004, manager Joe Torre assigned him that duty. After Torre left in the off-season to become manager of the Los Angeles Dodgers, successor Joe Girardi named Thomson bench coach.

Before the 2008 season was a week old, Thomson had become a Yankees manager. Before the game of April 4, Girardi was suffering with an upper-respiratory infection. He called Thomson into his office and told him to manage that night against the Tampa Bay Rays.

"I was excited," Thomson told me in a phone conversation. "But once the game started, I was so focused, I settled down."

Girardi stayed in his office during the game, but Thomson sneaked in occasionally to consult his manager. Girardi was too ill to manage the next game, and again Thomson took over. When the Yanks lost both games, Rob had to face some good-natured ribbing from the players.

Thomson didn't realize it at the time, but his two-game managerial career was making history. Jim Cressman, in the London (Ontario) Free Press, wrote it was the first time a Canadian had managed a major league game since George Gibson of London with the Pittsburgh Pirates in 1934.

Rob Thomson grew up in Corunna, Ontario, an avid Tigers fan. He had two older brothers, Tom and Rick. Tom was a catcher for a short time for Quebec City in the Montreal Expos organization.

Rob was a catcher, too. He was the Tigers' 32nd-round draft pick in 1985. George Bradley had scouted him and signed him for Detroit. After Bradley switched his front-office expertise to the Yankees, he guided Rob into that organization.

Thomson caught three years in the Tigers system, ending his playing career at Lakeland. It was there in 1988 he first coached — for manager Johnny Lipon. After a year as a coach for manager Chris Chambliss at London, Thomson left the Tigers to become third-base coach and hitting instructor with Ft. Lauderdale — the first of his 19 years in the Yankees organization.

Thomson cherishes his boyhood days as a Tigers fan. His dad, Jack, often took Rob and his brothers to watch the Tigers. Jack, who ran a construction business, was thrilled when Rob joined the Detroiters.

Now, Rob is a Yankee, with four World Series rings.

ORIGINALLY PRINTED APRIL 28, 2008.

ASK ERNIE!

GROUNDBALL RULE

Q If a batter hits a sac fly he is not charged with a time at-bat. Using the same scenario, if a batter hits a ground ball with less than two out and a runner scores from third how come he is charged with a time at-bat?

A This is an intriguing question. With help from Tim Wiles, Bill Francis and Gabriel Schechter at the Baseball Hall of Fame, here is the answer: The rule began in 1889, when a fly ball and also a grounder that scored the runner were considered a sacrifice. In 1894, the grounder sacrifice was eliminated, sacrifice on a bunt added and the sac fly maintained. When rule changes came again in 1908, the fly and the bunt were still there. The next alteration happened in 1931 when the sac fly was eliminated. It was restored in 1939 and survived the 1954 changes, but was redefined as a fly in fair territory. Through all of this, the grounder for a sacrifice faded away quickly, never to return.

BEHIND THE MICROPHONE

"ERNIE ON THE MIKE: He stood there like the house by the side of the road and watched that one go by. **"**

ON A CALLED THIRD STRIKE

Broadcast road to majors can be long

M inor league baseball announcers dream of reaching the major leagues. Most don't realize their dream, spending their entire career in the minors.

I had that dream when I broadcast Atlanta Cracker games in the Southern League for Wheaties.

Wheaties was serious about its sponsorship of more than 90 major and minor league teams across the country. The company and its ad agency, Knox Reeves, published a monthly magazine devoted to the broadcasts. Each year it staged a national convention for all its announcers.

The company sent an expert to each city, where he would listen to the Wheaties announcer and make a report to headquarters in Minneapolis. You can imagine the importance of this visit for each announcer. All of us strived to be at the top of our game for our visiting expert, whose critique might pave our way to the big leagues.

Brad Robinson came to Atlanta to listen to me and possibly determine my future. After dinner at a downtown restaurant, he went with me to radio station WATL to hear my broadcast of the Atlanta game at Mobile, Ala.

When the Atlanta team played out of town, I

A young Ernie Harwell began his career in sports broadcasting with 50,000-watt Atlanta radio station WSB in May 1940.

always did a re-creation — never traveling with the team, but staying in Atlanta to work from a telegraphic report.

I asked Robinson if he would like to hear the game while sitting on a couch in the radio station lobby, or would he rather come into the studio to watch me working at the mike?

"I think I'd get a better idea of the average listener's reaction to you," he said, "if I listen out here in the lobby."

The game in Mobile lasted 21 innings, ending in a tie because of curfew.

I broadcast every play, read a live commercial every half-inning and did my own station breaks. In other words, I did not leave my chair and was on the air, by myself, for 21 innings.

When the game ended and I signed off, it was 1:45 a.m. I got my papers together and headed toward the lobby to see Robinson, the man from Wheaties and my possible ticket to the big leagues.

I looked over to the couch where I had left him. He was fast asleep.

Did I lose him in the second inning, the 12th or when?

ORIGINALLY PRINTED SEPTEMBER 8, 2008.

ASK ERNIE!

ERNIE HARWELL ANSWERS READERS' QUESTIONS

WEARING PANTS LOW

Q Why do most of the players these days wear their pants so low they touch their shoes and you can't see their socks?

A That style started in the early 1990s when players began to tire of wearing knickers and stirrup stockings. It is much easier for them to dress in long pants. Uniforms have undergone many changes over the years. Ironically, the first club in baseball history, the New York Knickerbockers, wore long pants — much like the modern players. Since the Knickerbockers in the 1840s, players have dressed in shorts, knickers and long pants.

ASK ERNIE!

ERNIE HARWELL ANSWERS READERS' QUESTIONS

GEORGE KELL

Q What made George Kell such an endearing voice as the Tigers' play-by-play television analyst for so many years?

A It was a friendly style — laid-back, forthright and honest. He was never overly critical of the players, even though he'd been a great player and had the right to be critical. He had the background of a player, and the players looked on him as an authority on the game.

He let the game be paramount in his broadcast. He didn't interfere with it. He brought the game to the folks, where they got the idea that he was a friend of theirs.

Hall of Famer George Kell joined the Tigers' TV/radio team in 1959 and worked with nine partners until he retired in 1997.

Praise boosted this novice broadcaster

When Jocko Maxwell died in West Chester, Pa., at age 100 in 2008, I lost a friend who exerted a strong influence on my career.

He encouraged me when I was a struggling newcomer in need of a shot of confidence.

It was May 1940. I had just landed a job as a sports announcer at WSB, Atlanta's powerhouse NBC outlet of 50,000 watts, clear channel. Why such a prestigious station would hire an untried newcomer is a mystery. My meager experience was in print media — Atlanta correspondent for the Sporting News and six years on the sports desk of the Atlanta Constitution. I had never been close to a microphone. Still attending Emory University, I could hardly believe I had won an audition for the job.

Nervous and unsteady on my sportscasts, I worried about public reaction. Then, I received a letter from Jocko Maxwell, writer and radio broadcaster in Long Island, N.Y. He wrote glowing words about my show. You'd be surprised the power that letter exerted on my career. I was a struggling newcomer, and here was a real boost — confirmation from a sports authority.

Immediately, I sent Maxwell a thank-you note. Within a year he wrote this in his newspaper col-

ERNIE HARWELL

NEWARK STAR-LEDGER FILE PHOTO

Jocko Maxwell was the first African-American sportscaster and a chronicler of the Negro Leagues, often on WHOM in New Jersey.

umn: "When it comes to ace-high sportscasting, Ernie Harwell takes the eight-layer cake. In the short space of nine months, the Georgia gentleman has become the Sports Voice of the South."

This printed support strengthened my confidence and enhanced Maxwell's influence on my early career.

After two years of corresponding with me, he sent me a photograph of himself.

"Is my face red?" he wrote. "No, it's black. I bet you didn't know, did you?"

No, I didn't know. It was a surprise that he was an African American. We continued to correspond during my four years in the Marines. When I returned to civilian life in 1946, Jocko sent me his book, "Thrills and Spills in Sports," but after that

Jocko Maxwell, a sports writer and broad-caster, encouraged Ernie Harwell when Harwell was beginning his career.

1998 NEWARK STAR-LEDGER PHOTO

we lost touch with each other.

Then in October 2001, I finally met my friend. I was making a speech at the Hall of Fame in Cooperstown. As I entered the room, I heard "Hey, Ernie, I'm Jock Maxwell."

"Jocko," I shouted, "I haven't heard from you in 50 years. Great to see you."

At the age of 93 and in a wheelchair, Maxwell was lively and alert. After my speech, we embraced and had a long talk. Jocko told me something about himself I had never known. In 1929, he had been the first African American to conduct a sports show, a true pioneer. And as a sports writer he blazed the trail for Wendell Smith, Sam Lacy and Larry Whiteside, the three African-American writers in the Hall of Fame.

Jocko himself is not enshrined at Cooperstown, but he is certainly in my Hall of Fame. I still appreciate the influence his kind, encouraging words had on a struggling, unsure radio newcomer.

ORIGINALLY PRINTED JULY 28, 2008.

ASK ERNIE!

ERNIE HARWELL ANSWERS READERS' QUESTIONS

HOME TO OUTFIELD

Q Is the distance from home plate to the outfield wall measured from the top or bottom of the wall?

A Heather Nabozny, head groundskeeper at Comerica Park, answered this one. She says the measurement is taken on the ground and extends from the apex of home plate to the bottom of the fence. There have been many inaccurate ballpark measurements — even in the big leagues. (Maybe that's the origin of the phrase, "Ball Park Figure.") Sports writer Joe Falls once paced off the distance from home plate at Fenway Park in Boston to the Green Monster in leftfield. Official measurement was 315 feet. Joe's unofficial pacing was just under the 300 mark.

And now, a word from our sponsor

The announcer's strident voice demands our attention, "This broadcast is brought to you by: Morton's Cutglass Fly-Swatter, You get all the breaks, and by: Finkell's Fur-lined Syrup Pitcher, We always stick by you. And by ..." and on and on through a list of almost 20 sponsors.

No broadcast can happen without sponsors. There used to be only one per game. Now, there are many. Even after the billboard (TV-ese for the opening salvo), they keep on coming. There are sponsors for the lineups, stolen bases, pitching changes — almost any happening within the game.

We, as listeners, can do nothing about it. Airing a baseball game costs money. Equipment, announcers, directors, engineers — all kinds of production people are involved. All of them have to be paid.

In the beginning of baseball broadcasting, there were no sponsors. Ty Tyson, the great Tigers pioneer announcer, told me that when his station, WWJ, had Mobil Oil as its first sponsor in the mid-'20s, he made no commercial announcements during the game. "At the start of the broadcast," he told me, "I would say, 'This game is brought to you by the Flying Red Horse.' Then, when it was over, I would sign off with 'This game has been brought to you by the Flying Red Horse.' That was my only mention of our sponsor."

The first World Series broadcast was in 1921, but the Fall Classic didn't have a sponsor until 1934, when commissioner Kenesaw Mountain Landis negotiated a four-year deal with Ford Motor Co. for $400,000.

After Ford took the first step, other World Series sponsors followed. Then, the regular-season games of each team began to find sponsorships. Baseball soon became an outstanding commercial vehicle.

However, some club owners refused to air their games and fought to keep baseball off the air because they feared the broadcasts would hurt attendance.

Strangely enough, New York, the most aggressive of all cities and the center of world communications, was the No. 1 offender. In 1934, the Yankees, Giants and Dodgers joined in a pact to bar baseball broadcasts. In 1939, Dodgers executive Larry MacPhail broke that pact and all three New York clubs began to broadcast — something Detroit, Cleveland, Chicago and other cities had been doing for years.

Modern science now enables us to hear baseball broadcasts anywhere in the world. And everywhere the broadcasts go, sponsors go along with them. It's a far cry from the time when Ty Tyson, without a sponsor, pioneered baseball broadcasting in Detroit.

ORIGINALLY PRINTED MAY 26, 2008.

ASK ERNIE!

ERNIE HARWELL ANSWERS READERS' QUESTIONS

TY TYSON

Q I remember Ty Tyson broadcasting Tigers games, played away, that Tyson read from a teletype machine that could be heard in background. What years was he a Tigers broadcaster?

A Ty broadcast Tigers games from 1927 until 1942, doing many telegraphic re-creations. He was not only the first Tiger baseball broadcaster, he was the first anywhere. On April 19, 1927, Tyson broadcast the first regular-season game and was the first in radio history to do a full season.

Even before he was the Tigers' announcer, Ty broadcast University of Michigan football. He also announced boxing and the Gold Cup Races.

On his baseball broadcasts his laid-back style and dry humor won many friends. The Tiger fans loved him. When the Detroiters reached the World Series in 1934, Ty was not selected for the network broadcast. The oversight brought 600,000 petitions from Tiger fans who wanted to hear their favorite call the games.

After Ty retired, I would often take him with me to the Tiger games. On Father's Day, 1965, I asked him to do an inning of play-by-play. The fan response was fantastic. Everybody loved hearing him again. Yes, he was a true treasure.

Announcer Graney a part of many firsts

Sometimes a letter sparks a column idea. William Rayner of St. Thomas, Ontario, wrote that his hometown was the birthplace of Jack Graney, the one-time Cleveland baseball announcer.

I never listened to Graney broadcast, but I had heard glowing reports of his on-the-air charisma from his former partner, Jimmy Dudley, and from many Cleveland fans, including Bo Schembechler.

Graney was the first major league player to become an announcer, working for the Indians from 1932 through 1954, but that was only one of the firsts that made Jack famous.

He was the first player to bat against the pitching of Babe Ruth, and the first to get a hit and score a run against the Babe, then a rookie Red Sox left-hander.

Graney also was the first to wear a number on his uniform, the first ex-player to broadcast the World Series and the first Canadian to pinch-hit in it.

Jack suffered humiliation in his first major league training camp. In 1908 at Macon, Ga., he joined the Cleveland Naps as a left-handed pitcher. With his first pitch he hit Nap Lajoie, the manager and superstar of the Naps. Soon after, he received a note from the great Lajoie: "All wild men belong in the wild west. You're going to Portland, Oregon."

During his stay in the minors, Jack switched to outfielding. He joined Cleveland in 1910, playing his entire career there through the 1922 season. He was an excellent leadoff man. Baseball people dubbed him "Three and Two Jack" because he was an expert in obtaining walks.

Graney's roommate and best friend was Ray Chapman, who was killed by a Carl Mays pitch in 1920. Jack was one of the players who helped the stricken Chapman off the field. The death was a shocking blow to Graney.

ORIGINALLY PRINTED AUGUST 2, 2009.

ASK ERNIE!

ERNIE HARWELL ANSWERS READERS' QUESTIONS

CHECKED SWINGS

Q When did the appeal rule for checked swings come into play in MLB, and were the umpires in favor of this rule when it was first implemented?

A This rule became official in the 1972 season. Before then, umpires had an option of appealing to partners. Some did not welcome the change. Jim Evans, our expert on umpiring and the history of rule changes, joined the AL that year and remembers that his crew chief, Nestor Chylak, was very reluctant to follow the new regulation.

1979 PHOTIO BY SCOTT ECCKER

Paul Carey, center, joined Ernie Harwell, rear, in the Tigers'
radio broadcast booth from 1973 to 1991, when Carey retired.

ASK ERNIE!

ERNIE HARWELL ANSWERS READERS' QUESTIONS

PAUL CAREY

Q | Whatever happened to your partner Paul Carey?

A | Paul and his wife, Nancy, are living in Rochester and doing fine. He was a great partner for 19 years, longer than any other. He is the only announcer in big league history who also served as an engineer-producer.

Paul broadcast Piston games for six years and was the founder and conductor of the high school football and basketball scoreboard program for 35 years.

He was a true professional, talented and with a tremendous sense of loyalty. The only problem anyone ever had working with Paul: His famous "Voice of God" made all of us sound like sopranos.

PURELY PERSONAL

> **ERNIE ON THE MIKE:**
>
> That ball is LONG gone!
>
> **THE HOME RUN CALL**

Two near-misses on the funny pages

My ego took a bruising when I read the Yankees had an ambidextrous pitcher named Pat Venditte on their Class A Charleston, S.C., farm team. It was a painful reminder of another near-miss in my career.

It began in the fall of 1953. My Larchmont, N.Y., neighbor, Harry Gilburt, head of national sales for United Features Syndicate, came to me with a proposition.

"Ernie," he said, "our syndicate needs a comic strip about baseball. Would you write one for us?"

"I could try," I told Harry.

"I'll help you," he said. "We need a story line for a year, with 36 daily strips of four panels and five longer strips for Sundays."

My alleged brain began to whirl. I came up with an idea about a naive country boy pitching both right- and left-handed. His name, Ambrose Dexter, would be shortened to become the name of our strip "Amby Dexter."

Gilburt was enthusiastic. After approving and accepting my manuscript, he convinced his associates the project would be easy to market. I began to dream of readers all over the world praising my Amby Dexter.

My work done, United Features now needed an

artist. Because he knew many top-notch cartoon-
ists and illustrators, Gilburt didn't expect any problem. Submissions poured in, but Harry kept on
rejecting them. After a futile month, both of us
were getting anxious.

Then, an ambitious, young cartoonist named
Jack Davis came to my home. His samples were
fascinating. His vivid, energetic style won me over.
But Gilburt vetoed me. So, we continued our
search.

Strangely enough, Gilburt, though still confident
about my creation, never found the illustrator he
sought. So, Amby Dexter died, and I had achieved
another of my near-misses.

Meanwhile, Jack Davis, the aspiring Georgian we
rejected, is now a member of the Society of
Illustrators Hall of Fame. His first big break came
with the launching of Mad magazine. His artwork
has graced many movie posters and among his
clients are Columbia Records, Reader's Digest,
Newsweek, Pepsi, Ford, Indianapolis Motor
Speedway and the Super Bowl. Davis has even
designed a 25-cent stamp for the U.S. Postal
Service.

I'd have to say Davis did pretty well, even though
Gilburt by-passed him in 1953.

I had another near-miss earlier that same year.
Gilburt had bought a strip for United Features
called "Li'l Folks," submitted by a young cartoonist
from Minnesota. The syndicate liked the strip, but
changed its title. In its first year, only seven papers

printed the new cartoon, but in 1952 it was featured in 40 papers — on its way to becoming a huge hit.

The newly successful artist came to visit Gilburt at his home in Larchmont. Harry and his wife, Ruth, invited my wife, Lulu, to watch a Little League game with the young man. In that brief visit, he impressed everybody with his diffident humor. I was on the road with the Giants at the time of the artist's visit. So, I missed my chance to meet Charles Schulz, the genius who created the world's most beloved comic strip, "Peanuts."

ORIGINALLY PRINTED JUNE 21, 2009.

ASK ERNIE!

ERNIE HARWELL ANSWERS READERS' QUESTIONS

FIRST JOB AS WRITER

Q | What was your first job as a writer?

A | It was with the Sporting News. I was in high school in Atlanta in 1934. I wrote the editor of the Sporting News suggesting he hire me as his Atlanta correspondent. I had never written anything before, and there was no real reason for him to use me. Not knowing I was only 16 years old, he gave me the job. I continued to write for the Sporting News up until the mid-1960s.

So many memories from Fenway Park

Boston has a special place in my heart because it was the first city where I broadcast a major league road game.

In 1948, my team, the Brooklyn Dodgers, stayed in the pennant race until the Boston Braves knocked them out with a sweep of a Labor Day doubleheader. The Braves went on to win the National League pennant.

Now, the Braves are forgotten and all of New England loves the Red Sox. Old Braves Field is no more, but Fenway Park remains a centerpiece of Boston culture and a true tourist attraction.

The two stadiums were entirely different.

Braves Field had a huge playing surface. The fences were light-years away from home plate — originally 402 feet down each line and 550 to centerfield.

Grandstand seats sloped gradually from the diamond and even in the lower deck the players seemed a long distance from the few spectators scattered through the stands.

When the park was opened in 1915, Ty Cobb stood at home plate and said, "No one will ever hit a home run out of this place."

In contrast, look at Fenway Park.

Fans are right on top of the players. The famous

Green Monster looms only 315 feet from home plate.

It's a cozy, delightful place to watch a game. The cramped little park is a fan favorite.

Some top-notch literary stars have met the challenge of describing Fenway.

John Updike wrote: "It is a lyric, little bandbox of a ball park. Everything is painted green and seems in curiously sharp focus, like the inside of an old-fashioned peeping-type Easter egg."

George Higgins characterized Fenway this way: "It's too small for a ballgame, too big for a bridge tournament, too old for a shopping mall and too young for a shrine."

One of my most vivid memories of Fenway Park doesn't involve the Tigers. It's my broadcast of Bucky Dent's famous three-run homer to give the Yankees an exciting win over the Red Sox in the 1978 one-game playoff.

On that CBS Radio broadcast, I said, "There's a fly to left. It's a home run."

Later I gave Dent a tape of my call and apologized for calling it a fly ball.

"Don't worry about it, Ernie," he said. "That's what it was. I didn't hit it very good."

Another Fenway memory is a 1998 Tiger game I telecast with Al Kaline. We were discussing the peculiarities of the park and I meant to say that Fenway had a lot of nooks and crannies. It came out this way, "Yes, Al, Fenway has a lot of crooks and nannies."

Then there was the Tiger game when Willie Horton's foul killed a pigeon. Yes, something different and unusual always happens at Fenway.

ORIGINALLY PRINTED APRIL 7, 2008.

ASK ERNIE!

ERNIE HARWELL ANSWERS READERS' QUESTIONS

WRITING FOR SCHOOL PAPER

Q Did you write for your school paper?

A Yes, but that was after the Sporting News job. I wrote a column for the Boys High School Tatler — some name for a paper. At Emory University, I was sports editor and wrote a gossip column for the Emory Wheel. In my senior year, I became the paper's editor.

Ex-Tiger Boros battling tough foe

Steve Boros, one of my best friends in baseball, is battling multiple myeloma, a cancer of the blood.

"I've had four months of chemo, and I'm waiting for a stem-cell transfer," Boros told me from his home in Deland, Fla. "There is no cure, but people can live with it for several years. It's the same disease that Mel Stottlemyre and Don Baylor have survived."

Boros is putting up the kind of fight that characterized his career. He excelled in many phases of the game. He was a popular infielder with the Tigers from 1957-62. Later he was a coach, manager, scout, minor league instructor and front-office executive. To each of these jobs, Boros brought a special savvy and delightful personality. He is one of the most cerebral baseball men I've ever known.

The Tigers signed Boros in 1957 out of the University of Michigan for a $25,000 bonus. He played 24 games in 1957 and six in 1958 for the Tigers. In 1960, he was MVP of the American Association at Triple-A Denver. At third base with the Tigers in 1961, he had a fine rookie season until suffering a broken collarbone.

After playing with the Cubs and Reds, Boros managed San Diego and Oakland. His last jobs

1962 FILE PHOTO

Flint native and former University of Michigan infielder Steve Boros spent four seasons with the Tigers (1957-58, 1961-62).

were for the Tigers — director of player personnel in 2003 and special assistant to the general manager in 2004.

After retirement, Boros and wife Char moved from Lakeland, Fla., to Deland, where their daugh-

ter Sasha Schmid is tennis coach at Stetson University. Son Steve Jr. is a scout for the Yankees and lives in Houston.

Boros and I became close friends in 1961. In Los Angeles that year, we walked to the Desilu movie studios to meet two script-writer friends of mine. We watched Fred MacMurray tape an episode of "My Three Sons."

Boros had majored in English, and we had many discussions about books. He loved good food, too. When he managed in Oakland and the Tigers played there, I would have dinner with him — either at his home or at some fine restaurant.

Toward the end of my broadcasting career, Char and Steve found Lulu and me an apartment to rent at Grasslands, their Lakeland complex. I even tried a mini-comeback at golf, playing a few rounds with them.

Whenever the Mayo Smith Society invited me to speak during their spring trip to Lakeland, I always invited Boros to go along. He knew more about players in the Tigers system than anybody. And the Mayo Smith folks always loved his colorful and candid remarks about prospects.

Boros has continued an interest in literature and writing. He has kept journals of his seasons as a player, coach and manager. He also has used his baseball experience to write fiction.

Boros has hundreds of friends in the game, and all are rooting for him in his battle against cancer.

ORIGINALLY PRINTED SEPTEMBER 3, 2007.

ASK ERNIE!

ERNIE HARWELL ANSWERS READERS' QUESTIONS

WRITING IN ATLANTA

Q Didn't you also work for the Atlanta Constitution?

A I did, for six years while going to high school and college. My main job was editing copy and writing headlines and doing whatever no one else wanted to do. I covered tennis, swimming and golf. They paid me what I was worth — nothing — my first year. Later, I got a dollar a day, working on weekends or subbing for guys on vacation. Our sports editor and my mentor was Ralph McGill, who became editor and publisher of the paper and won a Pulitzer Prize for his stand on integration.

Today's books more common, better

Baseball books have come a long way. In the late 1920s, when I started to read seriously, a book on baseball was published about once a year. Now, they flood the market. There's a new one almost every day.

The earlier baseball books were player biographies — usually ghost-written by a sports writer. Or, you might find a history of the game, or a history of a certain major league franchise. The majority of these were poorly researched, mistake-filled and leaning heavily on old newspaper files.

Today's baseball books are much better written. There's usually scholarly research.

In the past few years, readers have enjoyed outstanding literary efforts. Two great ones are by Jonathon Eig. One is his "Luckiest Man: The Life and Death of Lou Gehrig," and the other is "Opening Day: The Story of Jackie Robinson's First Season." Also, the Babe Ruth biography, "The Big Bam," by Leigh Montville, is a fantastic read. Another well-received book was "The Echoing Green" by Joshua Prager.

The quality of these recent examples is so much higher than it was in the day when I took my 50-cent-a-week allowance and searched the shelves of the Miller Book Store in Atlanta.

The 2009 crop of baseball books is a good one. "Pull Up a Chair" by Curt Smith is the long-awaited biography of Vin Scully, the Los Angeles Dodgers' famed announcer. It's hard to believe that this is the first book ever written about Vin. Smith, the author of many best sellers, is considered the true guru of the sportscasting business.

Another popular entry is "The Yankee Years" by Joe Torre and Tom Verducci. It seems that anything about the Yankee players or managers has a good shot at the best-seller list. Books on A-Rod, Yogi Berra and the late Thurman Munson are currently available.

I also recommend "The Dickson Baseball Dictionary" by Paul Dickson and Bert Sugar's "Baseball Hall of Fame."

I want to mention another book I enjoyed immensely — "Starvation Lake" by Bryan Gruley. It's about a boys' hockey team in northern Michigan. Bryan's first novel is moving and entertaining, with many twists involving murder and intrigue.

ORIGINALLY PRINTED AUGUST 16, 2009.

ASK ERNIE!

ERNIE HARWELL ANSWERS READERS' QUESTIONS

WHY NOT NEWSPAPERS?

Q | Why didn't you have a career in newspaper work?

A | I wanted to, but couldn't find a job on a newspaper. There were no openings at the Atlanta Constitution or anywhere else. I took an audition at WSB, a 50,000-watt station in Atlanta, got lucky and landed the job. That was May 1940. Except for four years in the U.S. Marines, I've been in radio ever since.

Some suggestions to make fans happy

Maybe commissioner Bud Selig can concentrate his attention on the game's fan appeal. Here is my unsolicited advice.

◆ Change the starting times for playoff and World Series games. Because they end so late, baseball misses a potentially huge audience. The NFL has the right idea with its 6 p.m. Super Bowl start. Even a Super-long game ends at a decent hour — and still in prime time. While working on scheduling, why not highlight at least one World Series afternoon game? Many school kids and older fans would be able to see these games and appreciate baseball's jewel presentation.

◆ Get rid of body armor. It started with the batter's abbreviated shin guard, and that's all right. But the trend has reached ridiculous heights. There is no reason for a batter to wear protection all over his arms.

◆ Raise the mound. When the mound was lowered after the 1968 season, it was a bad move. As usual, the pitchers suffered with the change. Return to the 15-inch height.

◆ Expand the strike zone. It's probably too much to ask, but wouldn't it be great to bring back the strike zone that extended from the batter's arm pits to the top of his knees? Also, once the designation is established, demand that the umpires consistently adhere to it.

◆ Cut the volume on ballpark noise. I've had numerous complaints from fans about this. They would like to enjoy a conversation during a game and not be bombarded by loud music and other distractions. Signage instruction for "More Noise" has always seemed silly to me. Aren't the fans smart enough to react in their own way to what's happening?

◆ Eliminate the day-night doubleheader. I understand the need-and-greed for two admissions per day for a ballclub. Also, I realize that games take longer than they once did. But today's fans might appreciate the return of the true doubleheader — at least on a small scale.

ORIGINALLY PRINTED SEPTEMBER 22, 2008.

ASK ERNIE!

NEVER GIVE UP ON WRITING

Q | **But you never gave up your writing, did you?**

A No, I didn't. In the Marines, I augmented my $78-a-month salary by freelancing. In 1943, I sold an article to the Detroit Free Press about Paul Richards, the Atlanta Crackers manager, returning to the big leagues as a catcher. I also wrote a Saturday Evening Post article on Ty Cobb and sold pieces to Esquire, Reader's Digest, Parade and other publications. I was sports editor of Leatherneck, the Marine magazine, and one of their overseas correspondents. Now I'm just a Free Press man.

POSTGAME SHOW

Ernie Harwell by the numbers

Celebrating the digits behind the Detroit icon's career:

55

Years of broadcasting Major League Baseball.

42

Years with the Tigers.

17

Times he was named Michigan Sportscaster of the Year.

1989

Year he was inducted into the National Sportscasters and Sportswriters Association Hall of Fame and the Michigan Sports Hall of Fame.

0

Number of active broadcasters who were honored by the Baseball Hall of Fame with the Ford C. Frick Award before he was in 1981. Harwell was formally inducted into the Hall on Aug. 2, 1981.

16

His rank among the American Sportscasters Association Top 50 All-Time Sportscasters, that was released in January 2009.

1

Number of announcers in baseball history to be traded for a player. Harwell was traded from the Atlanta Crackers to the Brooklyn Dodgers for catcher Cliff Dapper in 1948.

9/29/2002

Last broadcast as the Tigers' radio announcer. Ended by saying "I thank you very much, and God bless all of you."

4/26/2008

Was presented with an Honorary Doctorate of Humane Letters from the University of Michigan.

5/3/2008

Was presented with an Honorary Degree of Laws from Wayne State University.

2

Games he missed in his entire major league career: The first was for his brother's funeral in 1968 and the other was for his induction into the National Sportscasters and Sportswriters Association Hall of Fame.

8,500

Television and radio broadcasts between 1948 and 2002, according to the New York Times

6,687

Number of Tigers' broadcasts, regular season and playoffs, during his career with the Tigers.

4

Years he served in the Marines.

1934

Year in which he saw his first big-league game: Yankees vs. White Sox at Comiskey Park in Chicago.

1943

Year in which he got his broadcasting start with the Atlanta Crackers.

1918

Year he was born in Washington, Ga. Other celebrities born in 1918: Ted Williams, Bob Feller, Betty Ford, Nelson Mandela, Billy Graham, Oral Roberts, Howard Cosell.

1941

Year he married his wife, Lulu.

4

Harwell children: two sons and two daughters. Gray lives in Florida, and Bill, Carolyn and Julie live in the Detroit area.

7

Grandchildren.

7

Great-grandchildren.

2

Older brothers. Davis worked in the lumber business, and Dick was a Civil War expert.

Index

About the author

Ernie Harwell was born in Washington, Ga., on Jan 25, 1918. He began his career in radio and television in 1940 and has been broadcasting Major League Baseball since 1948. He retired after the 2002 Tigers season. He has written six other books — "Stories From My Life in Baseball," "Tuned to Baseball," "Diamond Gems," "The Babe Signed My Shoe," "Life After Baseball" and "Breaking 90."